The Art of Self Confidence Applied To Every Part Of Our Existence

Daniel R. Brown

Table Of Contents

Introduction   8

Soul Seeking in to Self-Reliance and Constructive
Change   9

Constructive changes to Self-Reliance and
Constructive Change   13

Positive Directions in to Self-Reliance and
Constructive Changes   17

Losing Weight in to Self-Reliance and Constructive
Changes   21

Searching for in Self-Reliance and Constructive
Changes   24

Finding to Self-Reliance and Constructive Changes 27

Exploring You in to Self-Reliance and Constructive
Changes   35

Constructive changes to Self-Reliance and
Constructive Changes on the Highway to Success   39

Addressing Reinforcements in to Self-Reliance and
Constructive Changes   43

Readjusting your Attitude in to Self- Reliance and
Constructive Changes   47

Removing Deceptions in to Self-Reliance and
Constructive Changes   51

Dealing with Fears in to Self-Reliance and
Constructive Changes   55

Stress Management in to Self-Reliance and
Constructive Changes   59

Releasing your inner Powers in to Self-reliance and
Constructive Changes   67

Parents as to Self-Reliance for Constructive Changes
71

Discover your Inner Strength in to Self-Reliance and
Constructive Changes   75

Through the Loopholes in to Self-Reliance and
Constructive Changes   79

Relaxation in to Self-Reliance and Constructive
Changes   83

Constructive Change in to Self- Reliance   86

Bodily Responses in to Self-Reliance and
Constructive Change   90

Building Self-Esteem in to Self-Reliance and
Constructive Change   *93*

Stress Reduction Guide in How to Use Self-Reliance
Skills and Constructive Change   *96*

Stress Reduction Guide in How to Use Self-Reliance
Skills and Constructive Change   *100*

The paths to in Self-reliance and Constructive
changes   *107*

Exploring to Self-Reliance and Constructive Changes
110

Discovering Truths in to Self-Reliance and
Constructive Change   *117*

Acquitting your inner Powers in to Self reliance and
Constructive Changes   *121*

Acquitting your inner Powers in to Self reliance and
Constructive Changes   *125*

Hierarchy in to Self-Reliance and Constructive
Change   *133*

Acceptance of Change as to Self Reliance and
Constructive Change   *137*

Guide to Self Reliance and Constructive Change
through Soul Searching   *140*

In Hunt of to Self Reliance and Constructive Change
144

Discovering Resources, Guide to Self-Reliance and
Constructive Changes   *148*

Self-Reflection, to Self-Reliance and Constructive
Change   *151*

Constructive changes to Self-Reliance and
Constructive Change Through Meditation   *155*

Think Positively! to Self-Reliance and Constructive
Change   *159*

Less Stress, Less Mess: to Self-Reliance and
Constructive Change   *162*

Enjoying Life to Improve Your Life: to Self-Reliance
and Constructive Change   *166*

Fear of Change to Self Reliance and Constructive
Change   *169*

Realizing Your Potential in to Self Reliance and
Constructive Change   *173*

From Relaxation to Self Reliance and Constructive
Change   *177*

Hobbies as to Self Reliance and Constructive Change
180

Positive Thinking is the Key to Self Reliance and
Constructive Change   **184**

Self Reliance Can Help You Take A Vacation from
Stress   **188**

Willpower in Self Reliance and Constructive Change
192

Breaking Habits with to Self reliance and
Constructive Changes   **195**

Conclusion: **200**

Introduction

Constructive changes to self-reliance and constructive changes rest inside of you and all it takes is you to take some time to discover your inner powers. To get started however, you may need some help guides to encourage you and to help you choose the best practices that make it possible for you to make creative changes that guide you to success.

Before we get started, I feel it important to define what self-reliance and constructive changes mean. We realize that some people may struggle trying to understand the concept of this title.

Self-reliance is your independent willpower to discover ways that you can make changes. This is your autonomy or self-governing will to take charge of your life.

Constructive changes are possible to achieve once you take action. Using your self-ruler within you that are your inner strengths, you can change habits or behaviors to positive ones. Constructive changes mean to reform your ways to positive, helpful ways that become beneficial to all.

Constructive changes as viewed:
Practical changes that lead to positive results –
Change negative thoughts to encourage a helpful personality or attitude –
Changing unproductive ways, such as sitting on the couch for hours watching television to productive ways, such as exercising,
Changing poor habits, such as lying, binge eating, smoking, cussing, etc to useful ways by developing a positive mind, start soul seeking to find your success in to self-reliance and constructive changes.

Soul Seeking in to Self-Reliance and Constructive Change

Sometimes you have to soul seek to find your guide and self-reliance tools to develop constructive changes. Is it possible to make constructive changes? Sure, but the problem is most people are stuck in familiar patterns that developed while growing up.

To manage the problem and work toward making positive changes however, it is possible. You just have to be willing and do some soul seeking to discover your inner strengths.

Some of the best tools available online will help you in your search to discover self-independency and to make constructive changes.

to self-stableness and constructive changes rest inside of you and all it takes is you to take some time to win your visceral feds over. Sometimes however you may need a few helpful master guides to encourage you and to assist you with choosing the best therapeutic practices that makes it easier for you to make inventive changes that guide you to success.

Self-dependency is your alone single-mindedness that you use that gives you solutions you can select from new ideas. Your self-governing spirits give you inner strengths that you can use to find new solutions. When you take time to search around your mind, you connect with your subliminal resources.

Self-reliance is your independent willpower to discover ways that you can make world. This is your autonomy or self-governing will to take charge of your life.

Constructive changes will take some time. Using your self-ruler and inner strengths, you can change bad habits or poor behaviors to forward-looking ones. Making these changes means to reclaim your skills and resources and reforming your mind to think positive. This will be helpful and will incline you to gain beneficial aids to take control.

Constructive changes as ocular, when you make practical changes that point to positive results it helps you to remove conversion negative afterthought to proffer a helpful personality or attitude.

Changing unproductive methods and means, such as sitting on the lounge watching television hours on in to productive ways, such as exercising, thus you are changing unconstructive habits. Who knows when you make these changes you may find a need to change some other behaviors and habits, such as deceptiveness, binge eating, smoking, desecration, etc to useful habits by developing a positive outlook. Even if these behaviors are not a problem for you, there is always room for improvement.

Take a moment to go online and find helpful subjects. You will find   to self-reliance and constructive thinking that perhaps will give you the tools you need to reform those old habits.

Making changes for the better gives you something to look forward to. When you make positive changes, your conduct shows to others that you have worked hard at finding your success. In addition, good conducts encourage other people to follow your steps.

Take time to find ways and your guide to self-reliance and constructive changes. Keep your pace when you first begin changing your ways. This will help you be creative and succeed in your goals. If you try to rush, it will only hinder you from making productive progress. So take it one-step at a time.

For example, if you want to quite smoking or lose

weight, set up reasonable goals to get started. Do not beat yourself down if you fail the first time. Rather pick up your torture stake and carry forward in your goal to finding your guide to self-reliance and constructive changes. Look back often to see your progress, and give you a reward so that you keep that positive attitude alive, keep soul seeking and you will do fine!

Constructive changes to Self-Reliance and Constructive Change

We all have to think positive for self-reliance and constructive changes to develop. By learning to think positive, we can explore our mind effectively to find our inner self and strengths that will help in guiding us in the right direction. Positive thinking is our guide to self-reliance and helps us to make necessary changes to succeed in life.

Use your subliminal learning skills with thinking positive to find your true feelings to be successful for making constructive changes in your life. Stop and think about how you feel about yourself at this minute. Are you happy with the way your career has turned out? Do you personally like the way you look in the mirror?

If you are not happy with your career, ask yourself why not. When you look in the mirror, do you like what you see? If you are not happy with yourself, how can you make good decisions on your career or looks? We need to like ourselves before we can like what we see or how we can be in control.

Write how you feel on paper and how you plan to make constructive changes to turn them around. When we are thinking negative you cannot succeed, use positive thinking to make changes.

By thinking positive, you will be using your self-reliance skills, or other words; you will be depending on your feelings for making good decisions in making constructive changes.

When making good construction changes at the workplace you need to decide first is this, is the career you will be happy with? How can you change your feelings at the workplace to be successful?

If you are not happy with your career either try to find the cause or do you need to change you field entirely. Is your job to stressful; if so ask yourself why and what can you do about it. You and only you can answer these questions to solve the problem. Maybe learning to meditate at work will help relieve the stress to become successful.

If you are stressing your job, think, because you make money at your job, which is your lifeline this is important to you. When you choose other duties at home over your job first, likely you will be fired. You will need to make serious changes, since their job is lost and they will need to find other work. So think wisely, at what time you consider changing jobs.

When you meditate on the situation and focus on what needs to be done first, you will be relieving stress by getting one done then the second. Use meditation as for enhancing your self-reliance skills to help you become more constructive in success.

Look in the mirror, since only you can make the necessary changes to make your life better.

Using goals to plan, your diet along with exercise will build up your self-reliance to be constructive.

Goals are helpful aid that guides you along the right pathway in life. In order to build your self-reliance to grow on; think positive in making constructive changes for a better and healthier life. You can use the goals you made to come alive and stand out to stare at you while you express; you can make these changes.

Learning to rely on yourself is going to bring success in the future. You are the only one you can depend on to make constructive changes to be happier.

Use guides, such as meditation and goals to build your self-reliance for making the constructive changes you desire to make. Positive directions in self-reliance guides will help you make constructive changes.

Positive Directions in to Self-Reliance and Constructive Changes

Positive directions are our self-trustiness and worthwhile changes that we can develop from drawing from our innate abilities. When we learn to think positive, it helps us to explore and challenge our mind pleasantly to discover our inner self and strengths. The director will assist us with guiding our self to the road, success. Positive thinkers often benefit more often than negative thinkers. Since these people draw from their inner strengths and ideas, experiences, etc they often develop new solutions quickly to solve common problems.

Use guides, such as idea and principles to build your self-steadiness for making the constructive changes you desire to make. Acquirements to rely on yourself are going to awaken the skills that you thought had died. However, you are the unrivaled ones you can depend on to make constructive changes that guide you to success.

Ethics are our moral values and are helpful aids that act as conductors to take you along the moral passageway in life. In order to build your self-responsibility to grow on; think positive in directorial generative changes to improve and your life. You can set goals to turn up the speed process on making necessary changes that guide you to success.

Some of the best solutions to guide you to self-reliance and constructive changes are meditation and subliminal training. When you meditate, or deliberate and apply on what needs to be concluded first, you will be heart-warming stress by finishing your tasks on time Use meditation as for enhancing your self-reliance skills to benefit you become more constructive in clover.

If you are stressing over your job, sit down and contemplate. If your job is stressing you out, perhaps you need some success tips in dealing with your boss, co-workers, etc to manage for now. You make money at your workplace. When you embrace other duties and put your work aside, you request be fired. When you make changes, make sure you think through the problem carefully. If you make rapid decisions, it could lead to serious problems.

If you are not active with your career, try to discover new skills and talents you may need to interchange your field entirely. Perhaps you can take an online course to help you develop new skills so that you can get a winning job. For now, try to adapt to some changes that help you to cope with the job you have now.

By changing your thinking patterns to positive, you will discover your self-reliance skills, learning to depend on your sentiment for making decisive and constructive changes.

For now, go online to view some help guides in subliminal learning. When you learn to join your subconscious and conscious mind, getting them to work in harmony, your physiological patterns will flow in accord.

To explore your subconscious mind perhaps you can learn to write your feelings and thoughts on paper. Review often to see areas that you can improve. Do not beat yourself into the ground when you see mistakes you made. Rather, take it with stride and learn so that you grow, making constructive changes that are desirous to you.

Learn to take some time out for you. Use this time constructively. Meditate to explore your mind and practice learning from your experiences, learning and so on. This is the process of self-developing skills to guide you to success by productively developing constructive changes.

Get on top of the new age coming by focusing on what you need to do to achieve your success. Do not stop with one change; continue making changes to achieve balance. Losing weight requires to develop self-reliance, your will to make constructive changes.

Losing Weight in to Self-Reliance and Constructive Changes

Have you ever though about losing weight? This is one of hardest things to do. It takes a lot of willpower and encouragement from others. Losing weight is not easy. If you are overweight it can be bad you on your health as well as your mental ability to maintain on a day basis. If can be done in time with some patients. You will not lose weight overnight.

It is not going to happen overnight. This is a hard spot where most of us feel mad at ourselves, since we do not give ourselves time we need to lose weight. We strive to make it happen overnight. This will never happen, so it is time to get over it, get up, and put some effort into losing weight. The problem is most people want to lose weight, but they sit around thinking about it, rather than doing excises or planning a healthy diet that will give them adequate nutrient without producing excessive weight gain.

How can I prepare myself for these changes?
You will need to first decide this is what you want to and do it. It is not going to be the easiest thing to do. In time, you will notice that it gets easier for you to do. Therefore, you are going to have to give your self some time to do this. Patients is the biggest problem

with people wanting to lose weight they do not want to wait they want the changes to come overnight.

You may want to start an exercise program.
Therefore, you are going to need a plan that will work for you. You can visit your local gym. They can help you find what the best exercises suited for you. You will need to decide the best diet for you also.

You may start counting calories by trying the Akins diet or Jenny Craig program also. You have several diet plan options to choose from, so take your time to explore. It is not as hard as you think.

It will take some time to plan this entire out but it will good on your health. You should talk to your family doctor to make sure you can diet without any problems.

How can I lose weight by changing my habits?
When you are trying to diet, you need to change some old habits and replace them with good habits. Some old habits you might want to break would be eating all the time. You should only eat three different times a day, without any sneaking in

between meals. This is going to be a hard one to break. But if you reach deep inside of your and you have decided that this is what you want then you can do any thing that you put your mind to doing. You are going to make your self be active some way like doing some kind of exercising. This would be getting off the sofa and making your self walk, or even go to the local gym and workout.

It will have to be a steady routine every day, so set a schedule for 3 times a week. You have to do it or it will not work for you. So get off the sofa and do it.

Should I reward myself when I make a constructive change that benefits me?
Yes, you should reward yourself with each change you make. For example, if you lose 5 pounds in one week, treat yourself with an ice cream.

Once you have done it for 2 week like you have planed then you could take a few days off. So rewarding is good for you and would be ok, just do not over do it. Start searching for your guide today.

Searching for in Self-Reliance and Constructive Changes

to stop smoking and making other constructive changes

Have you ever wanted to change your habits or behaviors but could not figure out how to get started? You may had thought of making constructive changes without taking medications. Therefore, you have to look inside you to find resources that guide you to making positive changes.

You will need to retrain your mind, explore your mind and do something different by using new ideas you develop. If you want to stop smoking for example, perhaps you can explore your mind to improve your willpower.

What are some things that I may be able to do to help me change my behaviors?

When you want to change your behaviors you may have to decide first what kinds of things might work for you and try them, like maybe chewing on a straw, or even sucking on a piece of candy. That will keep your mouth busy. Nevertheless, you have to really explore your mind and set your mind to stopping smoking.

You have to decide that this is what you want to do. You may have to train your mind to do this but it can be done if you really want it. Add to your goals and plans a review list of consequences, include what smoking can do to you. How does it benefit you?

How would I search for behavior changes with in myself?

You can explore your mind to find answers buried in your subconscious region. You can also visit the Internet to find guides that will give you options. There might be some reading material that you can find that may be of some help, however it takes you to make it happen.

This is something that you have to do and apply it to work. If it were as easy as checking out books at the library there would be many people not smoking. Many people that want to stop that nasty habit of smoking but are unable to do so.

Why should I quite smoking?

The reasons for wanting to quite smoking are so many reasons. Some of these might be cannot afford them, the health reasons they are bad for your health as well as those who are around you. They stain your cloths, curtains, things that hang on your pictures, teeth, etc. This is a very smelly habit. Therefore, if you are able to stop you really need to consider the consequences.

What are some things that you might want to do instead of smoking?

Smoking is a bad habit you want to eliminate. It is the nicotine habit; as well, most people that smoke have a nervous condition. When you smoke, you are using your hands a lot of the time so you will have to find something to do so that your hands are waiting to reach for that cigarette that is not good for you. This can be done all you have to do is to apply yourself and do it.

You can start by developing your willpower and learning to like you. It is not going to come over night or in a week; you are going to have to work at this from the time you decide to stop until you are over the habit. The cravings will come back off and on all though your life. This is when you are going to have to use your willpower and continue to take control of your life. Visit the Internet to find more information on your guide to self-reliance in constructive changes.

Finding to Self-Reliance and Constructive Changes

Finding to self-reliance and constructive changes is easy once a person realizes what is bothering them and how they can make changes and be successful. When making constructive changes you need to know whom you are and like you.

You need to know who you are and how do you like that person before you can make good constructive changes. Find your inner feelings by using subliminal thinking skills. Discover any doubts you have by using your subconscious mind. Travel inside to see doubts, fears, and work toward removing them. Only you can see your inner feelings; and you have to decide on the changes that you can make to feel better about you and life. No one can make changes in your life except yourself.

Use guides to encourage your self-reliance to come alive so you can make constructive changes. Find guides that will lend you a hand and then set goals. You can learn to make good decisions, be healthier and happier by successfully knowing which direction you want to go. Guides can consist of a list of goals. Sometimes you have to discover online articles, CD's, books, plans, meditation, and many other things to change old habits. When you use , it motivates and promotes energy for success. Become a new person by find the guide for you.

When we set goals and write them on paper, it often helps you to see clearer. This is a great way to build up self-awareness. With your goals and changes in black and white, they will stand out to remind you they are alive and ready for you to take charge. By reading the list, you can reprogram your brain to think positive in making these changes.

Use CD's as for building self-reliance skills to make constructive changes. When we are stressed with no energy putting on a CD to help you relax and gain energy for building you self-reliance. It does not have to be one certain kind of music to give you energy when you are down. Music will give you a boost to forget about what is stressing you so badly. If a fast beat sound is what it takes to get you moving around than let it be. Some people prefer a low soft sound to pump them up to relieve their stress. Once you relieve your stress, your self-reliance will grow to make constructive changes to lessen the stressors.

Practice meditation to build your self-reliance skills. Meditation will guide you to relaxation for making better constructive changes in how you feel about yourself and those around you. We all need energy to make good constructive changes; learning meditation skills will guide us. By relieving stress with meditation, we feel better and have more energy to make good decision.

Exercise with a plan is a good guide for building self-reliance to relieve stress. With a plan in hand to keep you motivated, exercising becomes a challenge. Get motivated and have more energy to relieve stress with a plan for constructive changes for better health. By relieving stress it help to prevent high blood pressure, sleep more restful, heart diseases and m1ake better changes for a healthier and longer life.

Software programs will guide you to relieve stress. Finding the right software is easy by searching the Internet to build your self-reliance. There are free downloads that can be put on your PC to help guide you when your down with no energy.

Start today to build your self-reliance by thinking positive and using guides to make constructive changes successfully. You will be so glad you used guides to help you relieve stress to boost energy. Discoveries is your tools to finding your guide to self-reliance and constructive changes.

Discoveries in Guide to Self-Reliance and Constructive Changes

Discovering your scout to self-responsibility and constructive changes is easiest once you learn to like you. Once you learn to identify who you are and begin to like you, you will find that other people will like you too.

Prolific changes are possible by pulling up the discoveries in your subconscious mind. When you explore your mind, you often find your inner peace. When you find this peace it often comes from suppresses feelings and thoughts you retained over the years. Subconsciously you might discover doubts you may had in your ability to perform. Travel in your innermost mind to discover these doubts that link to your fears, and then strive to release these trappers to take control of your life. Only you can see your focal soul; and you have to resolve your complications by learning to like you.

Discovery your visual aids to encourage your self-reliance to prompt your vigilant so you can make productive changes. Find exemplars that command to lend you a hand and then set out to explore your possibilities.

Exploring your ethics, goals, plans, issues, and so on can help you reduce the stoppers that hinder you from making positive changes. Periodically you have to discover online resources, such as CD's, articles, and other sources that train you to practice meditation. Discover your scout within to encourage your motivate or intentions to promote energy.

How to explore your mind:

Every one of us is different. There is on one person alike, so you have to learn what works for you. Discoveries are what using your own self-reliance are about. The point is you want to make your thoughts clear so that you can see what you need to do to make constructive changes by using your self-reliance abilities. Meditation will help you build your awareness.

Shakedown or obtain under duress by practicing meditation to frame your self-reliance skills. Meditation helps you to relax. When you feel relaxed you will make inventive changes by thinking logically and reasonable. We all occasionally need to build energy to make excellent teeming changes learning meditation skills to command us is your guide.

If you need help with finding your guide to self-reliance and constructive changes, start by finding the state-of-the-art programs online to raise your self-faith by thinking positive and using guides to make practical changes. Breakthrough the steam from stress builds up to find relaxation.

Online you will find software programs that will captain you to mitigate stress. Discovering this software program is easiest when you search the Web. You will discover free downloads, including the neurofeedback software. Take time to check these programs out, since you will find amazement at the results. These programs are useful with guiding you to relaxation.

Team up with a plan. Plans help you to build self-assurance so that you find relief from stress. Plans promote motivation, which boosts energy.

Practice positive self-imaging, or meditation daily to build your hope. Start with contemporary discoveries to construct your self-trustiness by pondering over positive thoughts that guide you to constructive changes.

Discovery alone is   to self-assurance-interdependence and Constructive Changes, since you develop new ideas and learn to take control of your life. Finding your guide to self-assurance and constructive changes is cinch once you begin to realize what is irking, or displeasing you.

The basic rule of thumb to consider when seeking your guide to self-reliance and constructive changes is to find ways to build energy. Developing energy alone will encourage positive thinking, which you will start to see the steps you will need to take-to-take control. Explore you to find   to self-reliance and constructive changes.

Exploring You in to Self-Reliance and Constructive Changes

Most people search for solutions to make changes that guide them to success. Too many people fail, simply because they choose to rely on others to help them make substantial income, keep the family unit strong, and so on. Many people fail to see that looking inside themselves will help them to find answers too many problems.

If you consider that people down through the years relied on influences that lead to major confusion you will see that it takes you to make changes that lead you to success. For example, Wicca people decades ago were deemed as witches, which these people relied heavily on natural resources and used several herbal remedies to heal. In short, because these people were not like the normal society they were deemed evil. For removed, these people were gracious souls looking for answers, just like you.

Nowadays, Wicca is becoming popular, since people started to see that organics and natural resources benefit us more so than medicinal remedies. Instead, of persecuting or killing these innocent people known as Holistic or Wicca remedy seekers, we are now moving to invite them to tell us or show us remedies to heal the soul.

Today the dictionary defines Wicca as a sort of religious practice that involves organic-worship as well as witchcraft. This is far removed from the truth. As you can influences can misguide you. Therefore, you want to learn to use your own self-reliance to adapt to constructive changes that lead you to success.

Instead of banking on influences try to find the truths within you. Use your power of mind to discover your own answers.

How to use your powers to discover your own answers:

Start with meditation. Meditation will help you reflect on questions. Use rumination as to contemplate, and to consider the problems you face. Use your cognitive thinking to develop your creative abilities and deliberate through each question until you discover answers to your question.

When you learn to meditate daily, it will help you build your problem-solving skills. Explore your subconscious mind to build awareness. Enter your mind willingly to find existing learning, experiences, history, etc that affects your mind devoid of conscious awareness. In short, you have hidden answers within your subliminal or subconscious mind. Use meditation practices to explore and find your answers.

Only you know what you need. Only you can explore your mind to find answers and to build your personality, growing to love you. When you grow to love you, you will start to feel good since you begin to think positive and find answers to problems that guide you to success. Life becomes easier. However, you must continue your learning process throughout your life to get the most benefits from discovering.

Once you develop constructive skills, you will find it easier to make changes. A, you move along you will start to see areas in your life you can improve to guide you to success.

Learn from history. Take the information you learn and use it to your advantage. What you learn may help you to see ways to increase your success. Learn to develop positive skills. By this, I mean learn to reform bad habits that clutter your emotions. Consider your behaviors and habits. Review the consequences of these patterns that might hinder you from succeeding to your fullest potential.

Continue to move ahead until you develop constructive changes that make you feel alive. With each step you take you will find it easier to answer questions, find ways to make money, friends, and keep your family unit alive. Get on your highway to success by developing self-reliance skills to make constructive changes.

Constructive changes to Self-Reliance and Constructive Changes on the Highway to Success

We all heard the statements down through our life, such as if you want it done right, then get busy and do it yourself. Think carefully about this statement, since the notions are facts that all of us must consider.

Most of us have skills and answers within us that will guide us to success. Success however confuses people, since all of us have something different to offer that prompts us to go in different directions. Therefore, some people find it harder than others to find success, simply because they are in someone else's shoes.

All it takes to find your success is to get out of someone else's shoes and fill in your own. Very few people will agree that it is easy to achieve success. Most people sit around saying, success only happens to the lucky ones. This is true for them, simply because they keep this negative thinking, which hinders them from their own success.

Honestly, success is harder because most people fail to see how to get their success. They often rely on others to take them to the highway to success. The truth is finding your success takes you. If you look inside you and explore your mind, you will feel amazed at the answers you will find that you can use as to self-reliance and to make constructive changes.

Take time to explore you. Learn now how to get on the highway that guides you to success by exploring your inner strengths, mind, et cetera.

When you take time to explore your mind, it not only builds your awareness it also guides you to discovery. You start to learn from your experiences, learning, past, and other aspects of your life. You begin to put those influences that misguide you behind you and start to rely on you to find answers and get on your road to success.

The key is taking it slow. Rather than expect too much from you, or expect a miracle overnight you learn to pace it and discover inner truths and answers.

The fact is we were created with innate abilities and even knowledge. We learn by observing our nature, which helps us to see what we must do to live happier, and to achieve our own success. By exploring nature and its entirety, you will find that what you must do is learn to accept that you were created with an innate spirit that directs you straight to your creator. Once you start to see this, you will eat healthier. Rather than relying on fabricated foodstuff made by man, you start to grow your own food to live healthier. We all know that fabricated produces made by man are now contaminated, and is causing major harm to millions of people. Therefore, we have to take action now to rely on us to take hold of what our body and mind needs to survive.

What does this have to do with self-reliance, constructive changes and success? It has everything to do with it, since if your body is eating unhealthy, your mind will be affected. When your mind is affected, you cannot think straight. In addition, the world is heading to food shortages, epidemic diseases, and so on. So you see by exploring your natural resources you can get on the highway to your success.

Get on your road now by exploring your future, history and your mind. By exploring your mind alone you will build awareness, skills, and clear up clutter, such as fear, doubts, etc, which helps you, find your guide that leads you to success. Address reinforcements to make constructive changes.

Addressing Reinforcements in to Self-Reliance and Constructive Changes

Have you ever decided to change old habits or reinforcing behaviors that hinder you? Does it seem that no matter what effort you put into making changes, you seem to get nowhere? Perhaps you tried a few steps, yet all failed short of delivering you the results you desired.

The problem is hidden from your mind's eye, yet if you explore your mind, looking inward you will discover resources to guide you to constructive changes.

You must retrain your mind's cavity to explore and do something distinctively different by assigning new ideas you will develop from your exploration. If you desire to change habits, such as biting your nails for example, perhaps you might examine your mind to improve your disciplinary drive.

At what time you desire to adapt to new changes by focusing on your habit patterns, your behaviors you may have to decide firstly what may work for you. Once you discover what works for you, it is up to you to apply effort to make constructive changes.

You must learn to call shots to take control of your life. You have to train your conceptions to take your guide's hand and make it happen. First, start by setting some goals, creating plans and then working toward accomplishing what you want to do.

You can benefit by examining your conceptions or thoughts to discover answers deep-seated in your subconscious mind. If you need a hand, visit the Information Superhighway to discover guides that may offer you words of advice to put you on the right path. You might find a few reading guides or books that you can use to offer you some help. Still, it takes you to put forth effort to make it happen.

This is something that you have to do and implement it to work. If it were as easy as checking out compositions or books at the library there would be countless of people finding relief from biting their nails.

Why does changing habits, such as biting nails considered a constructive change?
We can consider a couple of outlooks. Firstly, if you are going on an interview to get a new job and the interviewer notes you biting on your nails, he/she will think that you are a nervous person that affects your decision-making and you may not get the job. Body languages, such as biting nails are indicators to help interviewers make a decision whether you may qualify for the job.

Secondly, when you bite your nails you are digesting germs that you are unaware of and it can affect your health in time. In addition, you downgrade your appearance when you bite your nails down the flesh.

How do I make changes to stop old habits?
Firstly, you begin with developing your willpower and learning to like who you are. Do not set up

roadblocks. Constructive changes do not happen overnight or in a week; rather you must endure to make constructive changes. Willpower is your enforcer and eliminator. When you build your willpower, you find your guide to self-reliance and find it easier to make constructive changes. Visit the Informational Superhighway online to discover more informatics or studies to help you find your guide to self-reliance in constructive changes by learning how to develop your willpower. This is your drive that helps you to develop self-discipline, which comes from your strength of mind. Willpower gives you determination to resolve problems.

You can change weaknesses, such as nail biting by developing your willpower and self-reliance today. Correspondingly, you have to look inside you to discover resources that guide you to forward-looking changes. Address your reinforcement behaviors to see where you need to make a change. Readjust your attitude to find your guide to self-reliance.

Readjusting your Attitude in to Self- Reliance and Constructive Changes

Concentrate what you must do to make changes, by stop allowing room for apocalyptic, i.e. predicting disaster by thinking negative. Instead, address your inner powers to develop self-responsibility to make constructive changes. At the time you become aware and identify who you are, you will discover inner strengths that guide you to success.

Prolific changes are possible by pulling up the discoveries in your subconscious mind. When you explore your conceptions, you often find your constitutional deepest peace.

At what time you learn to relax often you will start to release those suppressed feelings and considerations you retained throughout your life.

Subconsciously you may eliminate doubts that hindered your aptitude to perform. Take some time to explore your innermost conceptions to discover doubts that channel to your fears. Thrive on these doubts to release your fears to take control of your life. Only you can see your focal soul; and you have to challenge and look for resolves to minimize your complications that hinder you from arriving at success.

Developmental discoveries include your perceive aids that encourage your Self-reliance to make productive changes. Explore exemplifications that lend you a directive guide and then set out to examine your prospective.

Exploring your goals and creating plans can act as enforcers that guide you to lessen the stoppers that intercept you from commanding positive changes. At intervals, you have to discover E-messages or correspondences publishing on the net resources, such as CD's, editorials, and other resources that help you to train your mind. Look for guides to practice cerebration or meditation. Discover guides to encourage your motivation or intentions to promote renewed energizers.

Exploring your mind successfully:

You may want to make your thoughts clearer so that you can envision what you must do to make positive changes by assigning your Self-reliance powers. Meditation can assist you with constructing your comprehension.

Capture your compulsions by practicing cerebration or meditation develops your self-reliance tools. Learn to relax. At what time you feel a sense of ease you will start to make inventive changes by concentrating logically and analytically. Learn to team up with your mind and body to make positive changes successfully.

Allow your compulsions to help you with discovering your guide to self-reliance and commence to explore the latest programs, E-messages or correspondences publishing on the net to encourage your self-reliance by thinking positive and assigning guides to make commonsensical Changes.

On the super information highway, you will find a surplus of help guides. If you have computer with a

Windows Media program you have available neurofeedback and biofeedback tools. Visit your local dollar stores to buy natural sounds of music. Plug them into your D/E drive and open up your media. Click to play the hit and then request to view visual aids while you listen to the music. You will find to relaxation.

Relaxation is the top pick. That is you want to learn to relax more often so that you can develop skills by unleashing your inner mind.

The essential rule of hit and miss to consider while in quest of your guide to self-reliance to make constructive changes is to discover methods and means to build or renewed energizers. Developing energy will inspire positive concentrating, which you could embark or begin to see the ladder that helps you to climb to the top of success.

Discovery is another guide to self-interdependence and productive changes, since when you develop new associating ideas; you learn to take control of your life. Take action today to find your guide to success by readjusting your attitude. Remove deceptions to find your guide to self-reliance so you can make constructive changes.

Removing Deceptions in to Self-Reliance and Constructive Changes

We all need to make changes. There are no exceptions to the rule. When we make changes for the better, it often helps us to envision our road to success. The key to making positive changes however centers on removing deceptions.

Analyze deceptions shortly and think about the start of all our problems as human kind. The first lie is what leads to our misfortunate ways of living, not to mention the many bad decisions that people have made down through the years.

Deceptions are dishonest. Dishonesty is trickery that often leads to failure. This is because when you are dishonest you are fraudulent, cheater, pretext, and so on. When you remove deceptions to make constructive changes, it leads to honesty.

The openness you develop directs your life to making constructive changes by relying on you.

Inexhaustible changes are easier when you pull up discoveries in your own mind. Instead of relying on others, learn to rely on you by exploring your history, learning, experiences, thoughts, beliefs, et cetera and then move to remove any deceptions you may find.

Firstly, realize that you will need to remove any influences in your past that left impressions on your mind. Even if these influences did not leave impressions, your subconscious mind has stored and hidden information from you that you learned from these influences. The goal is to remove some of these influences.

For example, you went to school likely. During your educational learning, you studied many topics, and were influenced by many peers and teachers. What you do not know is during this learning process, you only took in 50% of the facts.

The remaining calculations are deceptions that you learned from misguiding information that someone failed to research, analyze, and find the facts to back the claims. What you need to do now is remove these deceptions to find your own proofs to discover your truth.

We all are subject to religious teachings, instructors in education programs, parents, their parents, their parents, and ... the point is what our parents learned from their parents was handed down to us, and so on. You see we have a pattern of influences that we must examine closely to find our truth.

Our truth does not mean to accept immoral behaviors or habits that cause us distress. By allowing room for this type of acceptance, you make room for cluttered minds. You want to clear up that clutter by examining your attitude, habits, and behaviors closely.

For example, do you agree to and act in harmony with beliefs, such as "it's ok to view sexually explicit programs on television, violence, et cetera.

If you do, then you have many deceptions to explore, since these immoral activities will only direct you to disaster. A lie is a lie. There is no way around it. To find the truth you must put these lies behind you, and remove all influences that lead you to believe these immoral acts are acceptable.

Take time this week to practice viewing health programs, learning programs, et cetera without viewing harmful programs that slow your progress from making constructive changes. Review your week once you complete this test and discuss with you what you learned and explore your feelings. You will inspire motivation and positive energies each time you adhere to these tests. In fact, it is guaranteed that you will feel better by removing deceptions from your life and mind.

Solely you can visualize your inner strengths to resolve your drawbacks by learning to remove deceptions. Take time to explore today!

Dealing with Fears in to Self-Reliance and Constructive Changes

Changes are doubts or insecurities packed with fears that hold us back from success. Authoritively speaking, many common people face fears that hinder them from reaching their top performance. The doubts or insecurities often emerge from the concept, change.

Most people fear change. They fail to realize that change can be rewarding. Changes allow us to modify our life to transform or reach breaking points that link us back to the past. These breaking points help us to make necessary adjustments, including constructive changes. The process allows us to modify differences to make amendments, and adjust to conversions, or constructive changes.

Change in all senses has nothing to do with fear because it only causes atonements specifically if you are honest. Doubts or insecurities require special skills so that you can adapt to the constructive changes. You want to start by building you awareness.

Visualizing some instances that focus on negative and positive thinkers and how these changes can break you or make you can help you to relate to positive changes.

For example, take a women struggling with obesity. She may invest in exercises and diets constitutionally to make changes in an honest way, yet as she progresses, she starts to deal with circadian rhythm, physical altercations, and mental disorders that might direct her with losing weight.

This positive change will happen if you sticks to an exercise routine, diet and habitually work to finish her goals. Only then will she gain benefits from her efforts.

Looking at a similar situation, per se this person, yet reverse to colorless changes to see what whatever may occur. Per see, she took her hindquarters backwards and continued to think negative. What is going to happen is this person is going to feel stuck, and will often resent her and fail to see her full potentials that could lead her to success. This person will likely develop a low self-esteem. This is because this person permitted her emotions or heart inclinations to take control. She left room to underwrite rules of engagements whilst dwindling in her negative thinking. She likely will gravitate toward binging, digesting foodstuff, feel hopeless, and at last, she will misplace her value or worth.

.Because too many people fear changes, solutions are coming available. Change is the process of adjusting to something new. When you transform your behaviors, habits, etc to constructive, it only brings you great rewards.

When you remain stuck in the same patterns, you only hinder you from achieving your success. In the previous aftermath, this example is clearly afraid and consumed by her, own doubts or insecurities of dismissal, or rejection. This example is agape of modifications that may guide her to success.

Terrified of her abilities to make adjustments, the last example will likely fall short of success, thus she must face her fears head on to make constructive changes that guide her to self-reliance.

We see traits of timid person with low self-esteem and afraid to make amendments that rightfully belong to her. Obviously, this person is terrified of differences. Therefore, we must face our fears to find our guide to self-reliance that lead us to make constructive changes.

Sadly, millions of people remain stuck. They fear the worst when they are presented with changes. This action only causes trouble for them and for others in the world. To make constructive changes you must look at the person in the mirror and decide what you must do to lead you to success. Stop at your local library, bookstore, of visit the Internet to find in understanding fear of success. Learn some stress management tips to help you develop your self-reliance skills.

Stress Management in to Self-Reliance and Constructive Changes

You have many options to use as to manage stress. It is entirely on you to take action and find your guide to manage stress. Here are a couple of options to consider in the meantime. You can look at stress as your enemy or welcome stress as your friend to help you take control of your life and reach success.

If you view stress as your enemy, well meet depressive symptoms, since they will be around the corner greeting you with open arms.

Stress is naturally available and on a daily scale, it parcels sending stressors to everyone's life each day. At most, some of us combat these stressors to minimize stress by taking positive action. Reducing stressors then is your guide to managing stress, but you must find your self-reliant tools to make constructive changes that direct you to success.

Not a single person in the universe can claim they do

not live each day without dealing with stress. Therefore, the key to success is learning to regulate stressors effectively to manage stress.

The majority of common folks think that stress is their enemy or an accident waiting to happen. In light of their notions, stress can be your best friend, yet all it takes is you to learn strategies to thrive on your newfound friend. In all due diligence, or appropriately and carefully considering, stress is a degree of prudent focus of subject that includes exercises, standards, established rules and so on that determines how you handle stress. Of course, these rules involve goals, plans, and action. Without these three rules, you will find it difficult to manage stress.

Stress works for you if you learn to manage. Most times people experience higher loads of stress because of injuries, death, illnesses, and so on. Of course, if a loved one dies you will have a grieving timeline to deal with, but learning to realize that the power is not in your hands can help you return to your life.

Observe stressors when it arrives. You will notice that

stress will increase at what time you are giving responsibilities, or expected to make changes. For instance, at what time you purchase a new car or home, your take on other responsibilities.

When you take on new purchases, you have to adapt, making changes to accommodate to new financial responsibilities. Then you struggle further when you realize that you must pay for insurance, home and car maintenance, and all that other good junk that comes along with adding more responsibility to your life.

There is more. You begin to realize that now you must make constructive changes to adapt and fulfill your responsibilities. What you had done is increased your stressor load that will in turn bring you more stress.

Constructive changes to self-reliance and constructive changes:
Logically, if you plan and set goals before you decide to buy a home or car, making a big decision that

could cause you overloads of stress, you would find self-achieving goals easier and find yourself reducing stressors, instead of increasing stressors that welcome stress.

The biggest failures in the world come from bad decisions, or people that fail to put their best intentions first. When you promptly add stressors to your life without calculating closely how these stressors will mount up, increasing stress, you only put your self in the way of heart disease, diabetes, high blood pressure, and all those other nasty words that make your life miserable. Learn to think first and act after you carefully devise your plans and goals.

In Search for your Guide to Self-Reliance and Constructive Changes

Searching for your guide by meditating to discover subliminal messages hidden in the mind to find your guide to make positive changes:

During the aging process, our subconscious mind

hears and observes things that it will store for later use, including negative learning. You may have heard someone in your history downgrade your abilities, telling you that you cannot do something, rather than giving you a chance to try. These negative messages hide in your subconscious mind, and waits for later when someone triggers them to come alive.

The brain stores these thoughts to use later when we least expect them causing us to fail. Negative thoughts that are stored in our brain and mind can later destroy how we perform in the future.

Learn to reprogram the brain to think positive thoughts by finding your inner feelings for self-reliance and constructive changes. When reprogramming your brain to forget the negative thoughts it will take time and practice to overcome them. The key to success is learning to make constructive changes.

Sit down and look inside by meditating to find your true inner feelings. Why do you feel so down, and what is making you so stress with life in general.

Writing your thoughts on paper will out to the open bringing them alive and active.

You now can use meditation as your guide to assist you with unraveling those negative feelings to encourage positive thinking. Learn now how to develop your self-reliance skills to make constructive changes that guide you to think positive.

Learn to focus on one problem at a time. Let the other problems go until you solve the first problem. Reprogram your mind by writing down your thoughts and feelings on paper. Review what you write and reread in a soft, low tone. Reprogram your mind to think positive by reviewing your thoughts and feelings often.

Use meditation as   to develop useful skills to minimize stress. Learn to make good decisions. Practice meditation and subliminal learning daily to improve your skills. Take time to find management tools to cope with stress, time, et cetera.

Stress when we permit it will drain us of our energy. Negative thinkers drain positive energy daily that could be used to restore their life. Get rid of the negative feelings and become positive to build your self-reliance skills.

Without sufficient metabolism boots, or energy we begin to lose control. Soon with no energy and control, the couch becomes our home. The more depressed we are the more we tend to gain or lose weight. Depression begins to be in control that could become deadly to many people. Getting control is very important to be successful with the way we feel about life.

With guides to help you stay on track and think positive, you will benefit as time goes on.
Your energy will pick up with guides to help lessen the stressors.

Plan an exercise program to boost energy. Use this as a help guide also to take control of your life.

Feel like a new person by making constructive changes that guide you to success, by relying on you. When you boost energy, it helps you to see things clearly. You clear up cluttered minds and start to see what it takes to find your way in life.

Meditation skills will teach us to relax as time goes on with practice. When we guide the mind and body to relaxation often, we rest easy, think clearly, and feel good about ourselves. With more sleep, we can make better decisions on relieving stressors to be healthier and happier.

Finding guides will help prevent failure and increase your self-reliance to making better constructive changes in your life.

Releasing your inner Powers in to Self-reliance and Constructive Changes

Successfully to draw from your own self-reliance you must discover your inner powers to make constructive changes. Using your powers will guide you to success in relieving stress for relaxation to make better decisions.

When we fail to develop our self-reliance skills, we often feel depressed when we find ourselves relying on others. We lose positive energy from negative resources also, which hinders us from enjoying a longer life span. Everyone needs energy in order to be successful with how we feel and live. When we do not have adequate energy we feel depressed and often causes health conditions to emerge.

Do not allow negative thoughts or depressive symptoms take over your life; sending you to the couch wondering what went wrong later. When we waste precious energy, it drains us making it next to impossible to think clearly. Being a couch potato our diets become uncontrollable making us lose or gain weight that can be harmful to our health. When our diets are out of control and we have no exercise, our joints begin to stiffen, blood pressure shoot up, high cholesterol increases, and we feel there is no hope for us as well as many other health issues.

Learn to get in control and relieve unwanted stressors that may or may not be controllable. It is a known fact that stress is the major factor for causing illnesses for many people. Thriving on daily stress is hard and most of them you have no control over. We can learn to manage and reduce stressors to make constructive changes.

There are skills that you can learn to release you inner powers for making changes to become healthier and getting off the couch. Looking in to find your inner powers take a lot of positive thinking along with some changes to be successful. Sit down and relax by listening to soft low music to help guide you to finding how you exactly feel about your life. Learn to explore your mind, asking questions to discover your inner powers. What makes me angry to make such bad decisions?

Write all your negative thoughts on paper to decide how you can make constructive changes for better health. Create a list of positives verses negatives and look for ways to minimize the negative. Ask yourself what do you have to do to become successful and why do you get angry and make bad decision. Write you changes next to the negative thoughts so you can relate back to them in the future.

Read these changes often to keep them in your mind for relieving stress. Reprogram your mind daily to make constructive changes that lead to positive thoughts. Practice focusing on making these changes to guide you for building your self-reliance skills to make constructive changes.

Use your inner powers to reprogram you brain and mind to help you be a new person in life. Making changes takes a lot of practice and positive thinking. Do not expect changes to take place overnight. Practice by refocusing when you feel those negative thoughts slipping in again and gain control of how your feel. Take a step back and relax to look the situation over and tell yourself to forget about the negative ones. Release your inner powers to find your guide to self-reliance skills that help you make constructive changes.

Ten best tips to boost energy develop self-reliance; make constructive changes, blah, blah---

-Exercise 3-times weekly, at least 30 minutes daily –
-Perform exercise routines that do not overload the joints

- eat healthy
- give your body vitamins, minerals, fibers, proteins, etc that it needs
- take time out for you
- meditate daily
- explore your subliminal mind daily
- find your guide to relaxation
- discover neurofeedback programs to help you find your guide to relaxation
-Start at the top and work down again, and put forth effort to improve your life

Next, learn the ropes of being a parent.

Parents as to Self-Reliance for Constructive Changes

Parents share some responsibility with their children to help them develop self-reliance skills to make constructive changes. You are the child's guide. Keep in mind you will have interferences. The road will not be easy, since you will have teachers acting as guides that will often misguide your teachings, as well as others to guide your child.   When we become parents, we also become to help our children build self-reliance for constructive changes. Children require to help them through the developmental processes.

Parents must guide and teach their children to build productive skills that benefit them as adults. Without guides, infants could not learn to walk early, ride bikes, and so on.

With good guidance, we teach our children new skills like dressing themselves, riding a bike, how to clean their rooms and even how to bathe themselves. We have guides to learn new skills and our children need guides to feel successful in their life.

Teaching children new skills takes time and a lot of effort from the parent. We need to remember to encourage them and reward them when they do something even if they fail the first time around.

If your child fails to put their shoes on the right feet, do you scream at them? Sometimes we must guide our children repeatedly to help them learn. Sometimes they get on the wrong foot, which comes from differences. In short, your child learns differently than you do. So show some patients when teaching your child. Learn to praise your child when he or she follows directions. This will encourage your child to try each time you give them instructions.

Build your child's self-reliance skills so they will have the confidence to keep trying. Teach you child to think positive and let them know just because they made a mistake that we learn from mistakes by not doing it like that the next time.

Help guide your child in the right direction for making changes that will benefit them. When your child makes a mistake, allow them room to choose their punishment. Help them to see the consequences that result from their mistake. Help them to understand why their actions or words are wrong.

Making constructive changes to be successful is hard for an adult; imagine what it is like for a child. If you fail to help your child develop skills to make constructive changes, your child will learn failure. Because our children fail once or a hundred times let them know, they are human. Humans make mistakes. Instead of discouraging your child, retrain him or her to help them grow.

Do not tell your child to avoid doing something he or she may enjoy because you fear the risks involved. For example, if your child wants to learn to jump rope, instead of discouraging him or her with, "You shouldn't do this. It is dangerous." Instead, let your child try. Give your child room to learn. We all take risks. Learn to welcome risks that do not pose serious dangers. You child needs coordination skills and jumping rope will guide them to have new skills.

When your child is succeeds learning the task of riding their bike praise them. Let them know that you had confidence they would ride with the other down the street. Tell them how great they do when riding their new bike. Build their self-reliance up so they will know they can do something with a little effort.

With self-reliance skills, your child will learn how to make constructive changes in their feelings about themselves and other. If your child needs to make some changes about how they feel about their teacher at school. Talk to them let them know that they can let it out and tell you anything they have on their mind. Learn to communicate with your child. If your child returns home from school with an attitude, rather than blow up and cause other problems, sit down and open a discussion with your child. Give your child room to speak his or her mind.

Parents as help your child grow in self-reliance skills for making better constructive changes in their lives. Discover your inner strengths.

Discover your Inner Strength in to Self-Reliance and Constructive Changes

Discover you inner strength to guide and build self-reliance skills in making changes. In order to making good constructive changes you need to know deep inside who you are and like what you see.

If you do not like the person, you see in the mirror, take time to explore the why-who-what's-when-how-When you do not like you, it leads you to the road to failure. Take a detour and get back on your road to success by learning to like you. You can't succeed in making changes and be successful when your not happy and feel good. Do not spend your time thinking negative. No one will like you, and you will not like you. Learn to develop positive thinking patterns.

Check your thinking to recompose your thoughts often to guide you back to thinking positive. Discover you. Take some time with you to discover constructive changes, you can make that guides you to success.

To discover your inner strengths and weakness; you need to find them first before you can make the necessary changes. Use your subliminal mind and search your feelings by looking at yourself. Check your emotions. Why do you feel depressed? Why do you feel angry? Take some time to learn - why - who - what - how - when - etc. This will help you discover what inspired your mind to think this way.

We hear as children all the time. "You can't do that, you can't do this." Those annoying voices clutter in our subliminal mind and stays there waiting for the trigger to hit so it can spell out, "I'm angry." The negative things you retain in your subliminal mind are something you want to explore often. The negative learning remains in your mind and appears later. Our self-talk begins to tell us not to try this career because we'll never make it or why try another diet you've failed so many times before. Soon when the entire negative self-talk that keeps popping up we begin to believe them. It causes you to lose interest, feel worthless, etc, yet you have the power to change.

Find and bring out these negative feelings and use them to guide and build on. Build up your self-reliance skills by changing negative feelings to positive. Make a list of all your negative feelings about how you feel. Now add to the list what constructive changes you can make to turn them into positive thoughts.

Use positive thinking to reprogram you brain for building your inner strengths. Keep your list of negative feelings and changes handy to reread as often as possible. The more you reread the list of changes the sooner the brain will think the same way. You can increase inner strengths by making constructive changes while relying on you.

As you reprogramming you brain and mind to be constructive and build on you soon notice how much better you feel. Making constructive changes will guide you to make better decisions and more successful for a happy and health life. You will have more energy and want to exercise to guide you for thriving on stress.

Thriving on stress is never easy for anyone but as you grow and you inner strengths become stronger you will find making changes will be a lot easier to give you success.
Making constructive changes will give you the success you deserve for better health and happiness.

Grow and be stronger by discovering your inner strengths as   for self-reliance and constructive changes. You will be so happy you found yourself and changed your negative patterns to positive influences. Go through the loopholes to find your success.

Through the Loopholes in to Self-Reliance and Constructive Changes

Climbing through the loopholes involve taking time to explore your subconscious mind. Instead of taking detours to abandon or escape negative thoughts, welcome them, allowing these thoughts through the loopholes of your mind to explore why they exist.

Consider all aspects of what is causing you problems. Use your negative thoughts to your advantage by thriving on the stress it develops to find answers to your problems.

Many of us dodge ambiguities that cause us stress. When we have this get-out attitude, it pushes our negative monsters back and stores them in the subliminal mind for later use. Later, when someone taps a trigger your mind will channel, spread out and hit you with the negative thought that often leads to anger, sadness, depression and all those other unhealthy words.

It is time to take action now. Instead of letting these emotions get you down, stop making excuses and do something about it. Unless you want to be an escape goat for the remainder of your life, trapped by your subconscious mind then take action now.

Become a mountaineer by hiking down the trail of your mind. Get out your self-reliance tools, including your rock, mountain, and ice climber. Take it to the top by welcoming in negative thoughts so that you can explore them and find answers to your problems.

These negative monsters in your mind develop from your past. When your mother or father told you that you do not have the ability to learn skills, such as riding a bike, and when your parents put off yesterday what you could have done that day, it developed a monster called, doubt.

You doubt your abilities when people hold you back from learning. Take action today and get those

haunting negatives out of your mind for good. You
have the power within you, so take time to explore
your mind and go through the loopholes to find your
guide to self-reliance so you can make constructive
changes.

Do not become those people that held you back.
Instead of putting off yesterday what you could
accomplish today, put the ball in motion and get up.
Explore your mind. Let those thoughts come to the
surface and let them go. Let go and let God is a good
practice. Use it to your advantage.

How do I get rolling?

You can get rolling by exploring your mind. You may
benefit further by learning to understand what
negative means to you.

Negative means:
Harmful – disapproving – downbeat – off-putting
(can you say procrastination?) – Pessimistic –
unenthusiastic – unconstructive – Woo, "hold the
phone!"

Did someone say unconstructive? Well, to get rolling

you must learn ways to develop and make constructive changes that guide you to your self-reliance and helps you to reach success.

What does positive mean to you?
Productive – positive – helpful – useful – practical – beneficial –

Review the meaning of constructive and decide if this is something that will interest you. Take a moment and visualize you in the moment. See you standing in the doorway of success and follow your steps backwards to see how your usefulness, practicalities, helpfulness, positive attitude, and productive ways made you a beneficial person that guided you to success.

Continue to analyze your life daily. Take some time out of your noisy, polluted schedule and quite making excuses to make constructive changes. Get rolling now, since in ten years you may find your self dealing with some other negative monsters called, Heart attacks, diabetes, weak central nervous system, nervous disorders, depression, liver disease, high blood pressure, high cholesterol...get what I am saying!

Climb through those loopholes and take action today.

Relaxation in to Self-Reliance and Constructive Changes

Meditation is one way to achieve relaxation. Meditation is considered mind-guided control because you are allowing your mind to open up by breathing and visualizing yourself in a relaxed state. Another form of mind-guided control is self- induced hypnosis. Self- induced hypnosis should be learned from a professional before you start practicing at home. Self- induced hypnosis allows you to relax by going inside the power of your mind. To understand the technique you will want to go online and speak with a qualified professional.

How hypnotherapy benefits you:
When you learn hypnotherapy, you will learn control. Most individuals feel they cannot relax even when

they try because the stress leaks into their mind. With self-hypnosis, you learn new skills to attain relaxation. Individuals who have phobias, fears, or other disorders often find self- hypnosis will help them through times of an anxiety attack. Specialist believe learning to control any fear will help build a stronger person as well as a stronger relationship with others. Self-hypnosis will also help control your emotions by learning to observe yourself and your actions before letting your emotions rule. Hypnotherapy is another way to relax when you are in pain. Individuals who experience pain from a disease or accident find self-hypnosis can help them feel free of pain for a little while.

Another reason to use a meditation or self-hypnosis is increasing your sex drive. Many couples have found an increase in intimacy when they learn how to relax and view their inner self. They can often heal their relationship when they relax and communicate. Relaxation through mind-guided control also helps improve your memory. You are taking the time to relax and review events so the mundane information that is no longer important is shuffled out where you are able to concentrate on the things that matter.

Stress management is another way of looking at relaxation through mind-guided control because you are able to learn methods for letting stress go. If you have problems in your relationships, maybe you are having trouble forgiving some one you can use these self hypnosis techniques to view your feelings, to find peace, and eventually find the way to forgive someone.

Individuals who try meditation find a quiet place to sit or lay while they let their bodies concentrate on relax and their minds take a relaxing vacation. Music can also help during meditation to paint the picture the mind wants. Once you attain a relaxed state and let the stress go, your body will feel better. The pain your carry in your neck, shoulders or behind the eyes releases when you relax.

Self-hypnosis allows creates more energy and motivation. When you are feeling better you often have more energy to do other things whether it is with your family or being more efficient at work. Our goals make us work hard, but if we do not take the time to relax and leave the stress behind it is difficult to achieve those goals.

Relaxation through mind-guided control can be used in several situations. You can meditate to achieve a less stressful life or use self-hypnosis to expand your self. By growing as a person, you can attain more goals and feel more contentment in your life rather than keeping the negative feelings bottled up inside you. It is important to relax as often as possible to have energy for the things that matter in life. Relaxing everyday all day is of course excessive, but once a day for thirty minutes can help with the quality of your life.

Constructive Change in to Self- Reliance

Changes in how to live longer and happier by living healthier is important whether we are twelve or fifty. Changes occur at every stage in our life. Some stages have more significant than others have. Moreover, it will cause transformations that help us grow into maturity. When we experience changes we can have emotional affects that are not always good, but changes cannot hurt you unless you let them take over your life.

When you cannot accept the changes of your body, you may become depressed, or turn to things like alcohol. It is important to realize you have friends and doctors who can help your through these changes if you ask for help. You do not want depression or other problems controlling your life or leading to poor health. You may feel that it is too difficult to get yourself out of a cycle of negative thinking and therefore you will not try. It is important to realize the changes going on in your body are just part of life and you can over come any thing you set out to.

When you relieve stress, eat well, and take problems as they come, you will live longer and happier as well as healthier. You cannot avoid problems instead; you have to face them because they will occur. You need to learn to grow from these changes or problems.

Communication is the best way to solve problems. It is often easier to ignore the changes, but if you can take the self- esteem you need to speak about your emotions and what is affecting you, you can alleviate problems just by voicing them. A psychologist will tell you when you start diagnosing yourself you will always be wrong. You know yourself, but you cannot always step back and look at the problem objectively as another person can. To accept change you need to have an outside look at what is happening to you on the inside. This is why communication is extremely important.

Tips for dealing with change include understanding the changes that are happening. Recognizing what is causing the changes can help you figure out how to solve them. There is not a special switch to turn your emotions off and on, no matter how hard we try to find it. In order to deal with the changes you need to find something to substitute the bad habits with in a positive light. It may take feeling positive to ruling out the negative way you have been thinking. Emotions often surface quickly when our bodies are changing. We can feel angry or happy in one moment and feel very different the next. We need to realize where these feelings stem from in order to correct them. If you are aware of yourself, you can improve your overall self-being.

For example, you are going through a hormonal change, your emotions are up and down, and you do not know half the time what you are really feeling. If you step back from the situation, tell the other person you need to take a few minutes to sort through the things in your mind before continuing a conversation chances are you will not use the angry emotion you may be feeling or the depression as a weapon.

You can step back, see why you may feel that way, and then explain to the person that you are not feeling yourself that you are going through changes and you need some space to communicate properly in order to understand the feelings you are truly having. Check your bodily changes.

Bodily Responses in to Self-Reliance and Constructive Change

Everyone at one point or many points in their lives may worry about aging. We all want to remain young forever and experience problems when we begin the aging process later in our lives. Adolescence experience aging problems because their bodies are beginning to awaken to new feelings as well as bodily functions that prompt signs of aging. Aging means our bodies are declining, but proper care can help we progress with fewer problems than not taking care of ourselves. We notice when are body changes and functions start to decline the importance is not in the realizing, but in how we handle this change.

An example is the skeletal system. The musculoskeletal system is usually the first area we are affected as early as thirty-five because we are seeing the daily activities as younger adults are catching up with us. We need to take care of our body and understand the limitations. It is important to continue exercising properly, but you will want to modify your routine to avoid damaging your body especially if you already suffer from a disease or problem. The muscles tend to deteriorate first because they are thin and very sensitive. If you have ever had a muscle tear or broken a bone chances are you are more aware of the injury the older you get whether it healed properly or not. You will want to avoid drugs, alcohol, and tobacco if you wish to have age with health. These abusive techniques will cause health issues later on in life. The best way to combat aging is to exercise and socialize with friends.

If you are experiencing problems, you will want to consult a physician. Some individuals experience eyesight changes when they become older needing bifocals. It is important to seek a doctor's advice for how to keep healthy during the aging process. You will also want to leave about bodily changes that you may or may not experience. A doctor can help you reduce the risks of heart disease and other problems that occur later in life if you take a proactive stand.

A proactive approach to your health is the best approach for eliminating health problems in the future. This does not mean you have to take the fun out of life. You can still eat the foods that may not be as good for you, but eating properly is important to good health. Limiting the intake of foods that are not as good for you is just another way for you to stay healthy. All things taken in excess can cause damage over time.

When you first suspect that, you are having health, problems it is very important that you consult a physician. Even if you feel it is more a mental health issue than a physical issue. Women who experience menopause have to deal with bodily changes as well as hormone changes. The hormone's can cause depression or stress if not taken care of properly. There are other health related issues due to depression that can occur. Depression though it affects the mind can also harm you physically. Physically you can feel tense, a loss of sleep, or even experience headaches and fatigue.

Bodily changes and healthy aging should be important to everyone because we all go through these processes. It may affect each individually in a different manner, but we will all experience changes during our life.

Asking a physician about the changes you can expect at certain ages while help reduce the stress caused by these changes. We all deserve to age the best we can and have a happier longer life. Building your self-esteem stars with you and your will to make constructive changes,

Building Self-Esteem in to Self-Reliance and Constructive Change

When you are growing up in school, you are taught words like self- esteem and confidence. As teenagers and adults, we struggle to attain self- esteem because we all want to be happy and view ourselves as something worthwhile. Personal remarks may make us feel undervalued and finding the way to feel good about yourself becomes even more of a purpose. Guided relaxation for self- esteem is important to make us feel healthy and to leave the stress behind. Self- esteem is important with healing the physical, emotional, and spiritual aspects of our bodies. Stress will eat away at your self- esteem and will cause us more pain than needed.

Negative thoughts will induce stress, feelings of anxiety, depression, and relationship problems.

Stress eats away at self- esteem because we start second-guessing ourselves, feeling like we do not do a good job no matter how hard we try, and it will affect our sleep cycle. Sleep is very important to our bodies. Some individuals require more sleep than others do and sometimes you can actually get too much sleep. Those who suffer from depression tend to sleep a lot, feeling lethargic and unable to gain energy. Others tend to go until they drop being to exhaust to get an entire nights rest. Stress will affect a person's life and eat away at self- esteem because you will start messing projects up if you do not have the proper amount of sleep.

In order to keep the negative thoughts at bay you need to find a relaxation technique that works for you. Mediation teaches a person how to live positively while helping you relaxes. Mediation allows you to take a few minutes out of the day to shut your mind down and find a happy place. Health is also important. The more a person has low self-esteem and stress the more they tend to eat things that are unhealthy for them. Having a positive and healthy diet is as important as learning how to relax.

If you feel yourself thinking negatively, try to turn it around to a positive thought. Try looking at the positive side of an assignment rather than the negative. Self- esteem is all about how we perceive ourselves, how we think, and how we react to others around us. Taking a small step at a time is important. You should look at one aspect of your life that is affecting your self- esteem and work it out. Take something that causes you stress and analyze it. Look at the problem and find several solutions to solve that problem.

When you take up the meditation technique, you will learn that a soft CD and thirty minutes will help you. The CD should be something you will relax to, something that will let your mind wonder rather than concentrate on the words. Finding a quiet place will also be essential. You might decide a yoga mat in the middle of the floor is a prime spot or you might think a dark room where you can sit comfortably is a better place. Once you begin your guided relaxation to self-esteem, you will need to think of things that will make you happy. It could be a place that you have visited that you envision to take you mind away. You might find concentrating on a loved one that supports you will get you to the relaxation stage you desire. Most individuals picture something to get them in the meditation state and then their minds wonder over what ever the consciousness feels appropriate. Guided relaxation to self- esteem is important when you are trying to leave the stress behind and find yourself.

Stress Reduction Guide in How to Use Self-Reliance Skills and Constructive Change

Stress is the leading cause to health problems so finding a way to reduce stress to live longer and happier is extremely important. Stress causes pressure in your life affecting your emotions as well as bodily responses. Most of the time stress is related to fears, changes in your life, or illness. Work is a high stress producer in an individual. Managing your life appropriately is important to relieving your stress.

Stress in small doses can be a good thing. It can push us to achieve goal we otherwise would not be able to.

It is important to learn how to reduce stress to live longer and happier. One-step is to take a day at a time. Do not get overwhelmed by the many tasks you have to complete. It is easier to take one task at a time when you are feeling pressured. You also need live to learn how to live with a certain amount of stress. The use of drugs or alcohol may seem to reduce the problem at the time, but you are guaranteed to feel worse afterwards just by knowing you are not dealing with the problem. You body also responds to stress by creating tension in your body. The tension will make your body hurt whether it is a headache or shoulders being to tense. When you let the stress become overwhelming, you will also lose sleep. REM sleep is very important to your sleep cycle and if you are not achieving this state you are loosing out on a great way to relieve some stress. It is a natural coping mechanism.

There are certain supplements you can take in order to increase your health, but you should try to relieve the problem before taking these supplements as you can find a more natural way of dealing with stress.

Signs that you are over stressed reside in an uptight feeling, feeling nervous, depressed, or impatient for no apparent reason. Having extremely negative thoughts is another sign that you are suffering from stress. If your emotions are in turmoil and you feel you are crying or angry all the time you may be suffering from too much stress.

There are also other signs that you may be experiencing stress. If you are forgetting things easier or finding it hard to concentrate, you might have too much on your mind and need to start concentrating on one thing at a time. Fatigue is also another sign of stress. You can feel tired after a long days work, but if you are feeling, tired all the time and wishing you could sleep all day you are probably experiencing mental symptoms of stress.

Many individuals do not realize the cause of their stress because they do not take the time to analyze their emotions. Instead, they ride on the feelings of the moment and wonder why they are feeling pain in their head, neck, and shoulders. It is important to recognize the symptoms and causes of stress before you can begin to heal. Remember a little bit of stress can be a good thing, but when you are experiencing side effects of the stress that inhibit everyday functionality you need to seek ways to relieve that stress.

To relieve your stress you should look into meditation or communication. Meditation allows you to explore your mind and find 30 minutes a day to analyze your behavior without having to concentrate on the problems at hand. Communication can be as simple as speaking with someone you love or speaking with a professional who can help you reflect on your problems.

Stress Reduction Guide in How to Use Self-Reliance Skills and Constructive Change

Stress is the leading cause to health problems so finding a way to reduce stress to live longer and happier is extremely important. Stress causes pressure in your life affecting your emotions as well as bodily responses. Most of the time stress is related to fears, changes in your life, or illness. Work is a high stress producer in an individual. Managing your life appropriately is important to relieving your stress.

Stress in small doses can be a good thing. It can push us to achieve goal we otherwise would not be able to. It is important to learn how to reduce stress to live longer and happier. One-step is to take a day at a time. Do not get overwhelmed by the many tasks you have to complete. It is easier to take one task at a time when you are feeling pressured. You also need live to learn how to live with a certain amount of stress. The use of drugs or alcohol may seem to reduce the problem at the time, but you are guaranteed to feel worse afterwards just by knowing you are not dealing with the problem. You body also responds to stress by creating tension in your body. The tension will make your body hurt whether it is a headache or shoulders being to tense. When you let the stress become overwhelming, you will also lose sleep. REM sleep is very important to your sleep cycle and if you are not achieving this state you are loosing out on a great way to relieve some stress. It is a natural coping mechanism.

There are certain supplements you can take in order to increase your health, but you should try to relieve the problem before taking these supplements as you can find a more natural way of dealing with stress.

Signs that you are over stressed reside in an uptight feeling, feeling nervous, depressed, or impatient for no apparent reason. Having extremely negative thoughts is another sign that you are suffering from stress. If your emotions are in turmoil and you feel you are crying or angry all the time you may be suffering from too much stress.

There are also other signs that you may be experiencing stress. If you are forgetting things easier or finding it hard to concentrate, you might have too much on your mind and need to start concentrating on one thing at a time. Fatigue is also another sign of stress. You can feel tired after a long days work, but if you are feeling, tired all the time and wishing you could sleep all day you are probably experiencing mental symptoms of stress.

Many individuals do not realize the cause of their

stress because they do not take the time to analyze their emotions. Instead, they ride on the feelings of the moment and wonder why they are feeling pain in their head, neck, and shoulders. It is important to recognize the symptoms and causes of stress before you can begin to heal. Remember a little bit of stress can be a good thing, but when you are experiencing side effects of the stress that inhibit everyday functionality you need to seek ways to relieve that stress.

To relieve your stress you should look into meditation or communication. Meditation allows you to explore your mind and find 30 minutes a day to analyze your behavior without having to concentrate on the problems at hand. Communication can be as simple as speaking with someone you love or speaking with a professional who can help you reflect on your problems.

Meditation is one way to achieve relaxation. Meditation is give aforethought mind-guided control because you are admitting your mind to open up by breathing and visualizing yourself in a sense of ease state. Another form of mind-guided control is self-induced hypnosis. Self- induced pain-kill or dullness of mind should be learned from a professional before you start practicing at home. Self- induced painkiller or dullness of mind allows you to relax by going inside the power of your conceptions. To deduce the technique you will desire to go online and speak with a qualified professional.

In the meantime, when you learn hypnotherapy, you learn to take control. The largest individuals feel they cannot relax even when they try seeing that the stress leaks into their mind. With Self-pain-kill or dullness of mind, you become versed new skills to acquire relaxation. Individuals who have phobias, discomforting fears, or other disorders usually discover self- pain-kill or dullness of mind will help them through times of duress.

Specialist conclude that learning to charge any doubts or insecurities will help aggrandize a enliven person as well as a stronger relationship with others. Self-pain-kill or dullness of mind will also help control your heart inclinations or emotional responses by learning to discern yourself and your actions before allowing your emotions rule.

Hypnotherapy is another way to relax when you are in feel grief. Individuals who experience feel grief from a disease or accident discover self-hypnosis can help them feel free of feel grief for a little while.

Some other rationale to use a cerebration or meditation or self-hypnosis is increasing your sex drive. Abounding couples have found an increase in intimacy In the meantime they learn how to relax and view their inner self. They can often heal their relationship when they relax and communicate. Relaxation through conceptions-guided charge also helps improve your memory. You are taking the time to relax and review events so the mundane informatics or studies that is no longer conspicuous is shuffled out where you are able to concentrate on the things that matter. Stress management is some other way of looking at relaxation through mind-guided control because you are able to learn methods and resources for letting stress go.

When you have difficulties managing relationships, perhaps you can sit down and look at you. Use these Self-hypnosis executions to view your emotional heart, to find or negotiator, and eventually find the way to end a quarrel with a mate.

People who try meditation find a quiet place to sit or lay while they let their body's center on collect you and their minds take a relaxing gone fishing trip. Natural melodies can also help during meditation to paint the depiction the mind desires. Once you attain a relaxed state and let the stress go, your body could feel better. The feel grief your carry in your neck, shoulders or behind the eyes releases In the meantime you relax.

Self-hypnosis allows composes more or renewed energizers and motivation. When you are feeling better you often have more energy to do alternatives things whether it is with your family or being more efficient at work. Our goals make us work callous, but if we do not take the time to relax and leave the stress behind it is difficult to achieve those goals.

Relaxation through conceptions-guided control can be utilized in several predicaments. You can meditate to achieve a less disturbing life or use self-hypnosis to expand your Self. By growing as a person, you can attain more principles and feel more equanimity in your life rather than keeping the negative feelings bottled up inside you. It is important to relax as often as convincingly to have energy for the things that matter in life. Relaxing everyday all day is of course excessive, but once a day for thirty minutes can help with the quality of your life net. Follow your path to success.

The paths to in Self-reliance and Constructive changes

Find paths to guide you in self-reliance and constructive changes that will help keep you mediated and pumped up with energy. With guides to help, you will reach goals and make changes to reduce stressors by making better decisions.

Using a path for success is a great way when making constructive changes. Grow and become stronger in self-reliance skills as you walk down the path to success.

Paths to guide us in building our self-reliance skills will help us grow in energy, and to thrive on stress. Positive thinking skills work as a path to help us become healthier with happiness in our lives.

Start your journey down the path to find your inner feelings before you begin making   changes with the way you live. Use your subliminal subconscious to search your feelings and the cause of your problems. You need to know the true causes for your thoughts before you can change them to be successful.

Grow to strengthen you self-reliance skills by finding who you are. Grow with positive thinking skills for a path to relieve stressors that get in the way for making good constructive changes. If you are not happy and feel that, your decisions are always wrong you will start to feel depressed. Give your energy a boost by using paths to make good constructive changes.

Grow with goals for the future to find you. Using goals and taking one-step at a time will get you another step ahead. Start you goals by making short and long paths. Short paths like losing 5 pounds and long path of 15 pounds will help relieve stress caused from the weight you want to lose. As you reach the short path with losing 5 pounds, you will want to work harder to reach the next one at 15 pounds.

As you work your way down the path of goals keep adding to the bottom. When you run out of goals, you will be apt to slip back to your old habits. If you should slip and go backwards, you will feel even more depressed with less energy again. Once you begin the journey to success, keep going to be a winner.

Each path you go down will help your self-reliance skills grow letting you make better constructive changes in your performance. If you begin to feel, you are slipping step back and refocus by looking the situation over. Focus on going forward by looking back at your goals, and how far you have gone down the path to success.

Finding the right path is entirely up to you and what helps to thrive on stress. We all have daily stressors that we have no control over leaving us to thrive on. Some stressors can be controlled and eliminated by learning to meditate with focusing.

Use meditation as a path to focus on relieving stressors.

Always look for the right path to guide you when down and feel that stress is taking control. Stress is the major cause for many illnesses that drains our body's energy that causes us to fail. With no energy, you fail at making good decisions because you are not able to focus. Do not let stress drain you to the point that all you want to do is lay around doing nothing.

Additional support:
Practice -
Self-hypnosis allows creates more energy and encouragements. When you are feeling improved you often have more hydroelectrically energies to do other things whether it is with your family or becoming more efficient at assign. Our principles make us assign hard, but if we do not take the time to relax and leave the stress behind it is backbreaking to achieve those goals.

Exploring to Self-Reliance and Constructive Changes

Exploring your mind will help you find answers to problems. When you take time to explore your mind you find old learning tools that you can use to build a full workman kit to have all the tools you need to take action in making constructive changes.

Get started with exploring your gutter or subconscious mind. Take a stroll down memory lane to discover what you know. When we are stressed and feeling like it is the end of time we lose control and stress takes over.

Stress is the main cause for many health problems that cause us pain and depression. Making the stroll down memory lane, will help to relieve stress by bring it out into the open? On your exploring trip write down, what you discover and how you feel about them. When you write things on paper, it will help to guide you in making constructive changes where they are needed to build your self-reliance up for a healthier life in the future.

Become healthier by exploring to find the guide that will help you thrive on stress that we have no control of. When you explore and find stressors that can be controlled use it to guide you to relieving them for success.

When we feel we have failed and cannot do things as we explore our lives use other guides to help relieve them. Explore your feelings to find guides for success by rereading what you found on your exploration trip. Make constructive changes by using your tool kit to think positive for good results.

Restock (reprogram) your tool kit (brain) to think positive thoughts as you decide on what changes need to be done. Write them down along with your findings on the trip down memory lane. Again writing your changes will let them stare back at you so you can keep them handy. Reread these changes often to restock the tool kit letting it know that you are serious.

By rereading your changes often, you can restock the brain to forget the negative findings and bring out the positive ones. Reprogram the brain to give you a new guide for making constructive changes a success.

There will be times when the brain pulls up something letting your self-talk to think negative again. When they pop up and you feel like your failing again look back at your findings to focus on how much stronger you've become by exploring and using guides.

Do not let your original findings step in and take over again. Stay one-step ahead of old habits by focusing on your new self-reliance skills for making constructive changes.

It may take some time to reprogram your tool kit with new findings but it will come in time. Have faith in yourself with all the new strengths you gained in self-reliance skills. With each success, you will relieve more stress for making changes that are more constructive.

With the new increase in energy, you are going to have been sure to explore a new exercise plan for better health changes. Your going to need a way to use up your energy that your don't know what to do with. Exercising will help guide you to staying healthy and happy with all the success you have now found.

Exercising will help prevent diseases as well as giving you relief for thriving on stress that is uncontrollable. Without exercise in our busy schedules, we become sore from stiff joints and aging.

With all the new excitement, you have found by exploring and using guides for success you are going to be a new person. Enjoy your findings for self-reliance and constructive changes.

Positive Directions

Positive thinking is powerful. Thinking positive allows us to discover who we really are, and identify the strengths that set us apart from others. People who think positively are able quickly come up with solutions to the problems they face in life. Positive thinking empowers us to come to believe in ourselves and make meaningful and constructive changes in our lives. When you learn to rely on yourself, you will be pleasantly surprised by the skills that you have that you did not even realize you possessed.

Ethics play an important role in building self-reliance. Your beliefs play an important role in how you feel about yourself and how you react to the world around your. The things that you believe in can help guide you along the path to self-reliance. Through positive thinking your ideas, principles, and ethical beliefs can guide you toward making the positive constructive changes that come from increased self-reliance.

Meditation and subliminal training can help you achieve your goal of accomplishing self-reliance and implementing constructive changes in your life. The key to successful meditation is to focus your thoughts and energy on the most pressing matters you are facing, so that you can deal better with the environmental stressors in your daily life.

For example, if your job is a source of stress for you, contemplate on what would need to change for you to experience less job-related stress. Think through the causes of your workplace stress, and allow ideas for positive change to come through meditation. Do not act rashly, for you may cause more harm than benefit to your situation by doing so. Instead, slow down and meditate until you come up with a beneficial solution.

Maybe your meditation will reveal that your career is not the right one for you. If this is the case, start working on discovering what options might be better for you. Start directing energy toward discovering where your talents lie, and cultivating new skills that will enable you to choose a different career path. In other words, accept the negative truths about your situation and come up with positive steps you can take toward reaching a workable, long-lasting solution to your problem. New skills and talents you may need to interchange your field entirely. Perhaps you can take an online course to help you develop new skills so that you can get a winning job. This is an example of implementing positive constructive change through becoming self-reliant.

In addition to meditating, you may also find subliminal learning to be beneficial. Many online resources can help guide you toward joining both your subconscious and conscious mind so they are working in harmony. One way of exploring your subconscious mind is write your thoughts and feelings down on paper. This will help you become more self-aware, as well as increase your ability to track the progress you are making toward becoming more self-reliant and positive.

It is also important to take time out for yourself. Meditation can help you relax and deal with stress. Learning to cope with stress is an important aspect of introducing constructive change into your daily life. You owe it to yourself by focusing on the things you need to do to achieve success. Continuous change and improvement will help you achieve balance and happiness throughout all aspects of your life.

Discovering Truths in to Self-Reliance and Constructive Change

When we fail to develop our self-reliance skills, we often feel depressed In the meantime, we find ourselves relying on others. We lose positive energy from negative resources also, which block us from feeling contentment a longer life compass.

The mind is our power, strength, and gives us energy however; it takes us to note the transactions. Most times people feel their strengths, yet fail to connect with their feelings. Often these feelings are dismissed. This action leads to problem sees failing to learn the body and mind will only cause you anxiety and panic.

Power is our authority. Power helps us to stay in control, while influences our lives as well as others around us. Our power provides us strength to go on in life, while delivering energy, motivation, force and might to continue. If you consider power in full light and learn to accept after discovering your power, you may find a peace of mind.

We can consider many issues that cause stress, but overall it will boil down to one problem, if you learn to communicate with self and others, you will soon find new discoveries. Thus, open your mind.

Communication is the process of sending messages. When you start sending messages, you learn new things. Once you learn new things, the mind starts to open and feels free to explore. Let your mind explore.

Communication is also announcements that exchange ideas, while interacting with sources within our out. Communication transmits signals and information while transferring ideas. If you want to learn more about self, e.g. you would consult with your mind and pull up resources to help you learn.

If you fail to better self and learn self you will live with doubts, fear, guilt, anger, and the like and often feel anxiety and panic. Therefore, mind start exploring now to eliminate stressors, and stress. Stressors come from experiences, activities, and situations. Thus, start thinking of your situation, while examine your experiences and activities to see where you induce your own anxiety and panic.

Become a friend to stress and watch how it becomes a friend to you. Strain is often placed on the mind when stress occurs, simply because the person does not weigh out consequences, facts, ideas, reality, and the like. If you continue to strain the mind, you will find many times in your life when you feel anxious or panicky.

Overall, you must understand that it is impossible to get rid of anxiety and panic, however it is possible to minimize the experiences. Still, you have to open that unconstructive mind and allow it to explore the possibilities.

If you go around telling self that you will never discover who you are, thus expect never, since likely you will not discover. Thus, tell your mind that you want to discover new ideas that can help you to eliminate anxiety and panic and watch how the mind responds.

Read these changes often to keep them in your mind for relieving stress. Reprogram your mind cyclic to make constructive changes that lead to positive considerations. Practice focusing on making these changes to guide you for constructing your self-reliance skills to make constructive changes.

Write all your negative thoughts on paper to decide how you could make constructive changes for better health. Create a want list of certainties verses antagonistic and look for ways to minimize the negative. Ask yourself what do you have to do to become successful and why do you get angry and make bad decision. Write you changes next to the negative thoughts so you could relate back to them in the future.

Acquitting your inner Powers in to Self reliance and Constructive Changes

Acquitting your inner powers in for self-reliance and constructive changes will help relieve stress for making better decisions. Become happier and more successful in making constructive changes with guides. When you learn to accept the things you cannot change and take action to control what you can, it helps you to see what you need to do to improve your life.

Looking twice and seeing double visions will give you twice as much success to reliving stress. Stress will make us feel like we are seeing double at times. Stress can take over and be in control causing us to feel like a lost cause.

Use guides to help you feel less stressed and gain control for a more normal healthy life. Make a list of things you feel that are trying to take control such as bad habits, overeating, even your family.

Use double vision guides to help you relieve what stress you can and to thrive on the others. Write what stressors you have both uncontrollable and controllable ones. Create a list for each item and then estimate and then create to thrive on stress.

Take control and eliminate as many stressors as possible by making good constructive changes. When positive thinking through self-talking it will help you to decide what is the best way to eliminate and rid the controllable stressors. Focus on one item at a time for making the best decisions.

With positive thinking and your self-reliance, skills make changes to relieve the stress caused from all the uncontrollable items. Read your list daily to remind you of what you need to do to make constructive changes. Listing your changes that need to be done so you can read them often will help make the changes easier.

Make better decisions by learning to meditate for relaxation to relieve stress. Stress will
cause us to get less sleep, eat differently, pick up bad habits, plus many other things
When we learn to meditate or focus, we can think better, get more sleep, control our diets, and break bad habits.

Use positive thinking skills and meditating with focusing will help make constructive changes more successful. When you focus on one item at a time with thinking positive, you can make better decisions that will build up your self-reliance skills. You succeed when you take positive steps and work hard.

We often feel like a failure when our self-esteem is dropping because of overwhelming stress. When we fail to rely on ourselves, it often slows our performance and we do not feel good.

Having good strong self-reliance skills are important to succeed for a longer life.

As each stressor is relieved or eliminated our self-reliance will become stronger and more reliable for making better decisions. In order to make good constructive changes we need to have the skills for making good decisions.

Build by using guides to help you find yourself to relieve and thrive on stress. You will grow and become stronger as each stressor if lifted off your shoulders. You will notice that you do not become angry as often or worried about something you have no control over as you learn to thrive and eliminate stress.

Do not expect to notice changes right away. It takes some time to develop working skills, since you have to learn about you and what you know. Take time to practice using your self-reliance skills by focusing and using guides to help you. You can and will succeed with practice and using guides.

Meditation with focusing, guides, and growing stronger will get you a long way building your self-reliance in constructive changes.

Acquitting your inner Powers in to Self reliance and Constructive Changes

Acquitting your inner powers in for self-reliance and constructive changes will help relieve stress for making better decisions. Become happier and more successful in making constructive changes with guides. When you learn to accept the things you cannot change and take action to control what you can, it helps you to see what you need to do to improve your life.

Looking twice and seeing double visions will give you twice as much success to reliving stress. Stress will make us feel like we are seeing double at times. Stress can take over and be in control causing us to feel like a lost cause.

Use guides to help you feel less stressed and gain control for a more normal healthy life. Make a list of things you feel that are trying to take control such as bad habits, overeating, even your family.

Use double vision guides to help you relieve what stress you can and to thrive on the others. Write what stressors you have both uncontrollable and controllable ones. Create a list for each item and then estimate and then create to thrive on stress.

Take control and eliminate as many stressors as possible by making good constructive changes. When positive thinking through self-talking it will help you to decide what is the best way to eliminate and rid the controllable stressors. Focus on one item at a time for making the best decisions.

With positive thinking and your self-reliance, skills make changes to relieve the stress caused from all the uncontrollable items. Read your list daily to remind you of what you need to do to make constructive changes. Listing your changes that need to be done so you can read them often will help make the changes easier.

Make better decisions by learning to meditate for relaxation to relieve stress. Stress will
cause us to get less sleep, eat differently, pick up bad habits, plus many other things
When we learn to meditate or focus, we can think better, get more sleep, control our diets, and break bad habits.

Use positive thinking skills and meditating with focusing will help make constructive changes more successful. When you focus on one item at a time with thinking positive, you can make better decisions that will build up your self-reliance skills. You succeed when you take positive steps and work hard.

We often feel like a failure when our self-esteem is dropping because of overwhelming stress. When we fail to rely on ourselves, it often slows our performance and we do not feel good.

Having good strong self-reliance skills are important to succeed for a longer life.

As each stressor is relieved or eliminated our self-reliance will become stronger and more reliable for making better decisions. In order to make good constructive changes we need to have the skills for making good decisions.

Build by using guides to help you find yourself to relieve and thrive on stress. You will grow and become stronger as each stressor if lifted off your shoulders. You will notice that you do not become angry as often or worried about something you have no control over as you learn to thrive and eliminate stress.

Do not expect to notice changes right away. It takes some time to develop working skills, since you have to learn about you and what you know. Take time to practice using your self-reliance skills by focusing and using guides to help you. You can and will succeed with practice and using guides.

Meditation with focusing, guides, and growing stronger will get you a long way building your self-reliance in constructive changes.

The way you address to stress factors in on how you feel. If you react to stress in negative light, thus it could advance to or depression. Stress is a part of life and hits us every single day we live. There is no none of us can escape or take a detour to avoid stress. Stress overall is changes small and large in which you must regulate to its actions. Most people believe stress is a negative act. However, stress can assign in your favor. Stress coming from injury, illnesses, and death can also be, turned in positive influences.

If you buy a new vehicle and or home, it can cause strain. The stress arrives from arrearages and responsibility increase. The upside is you have reliability, secured, and a transportation or vehicle to call your own. The best solution before purchasing a new home or vehicle is commanding sure you have the revenue to pay your way out of debt. My philosophy of buying homes is you never own it. Even if you pay off the home, you pay the city government, state, and federal taxes for the course of your life span. Therefore, consider that the debt is lasting, in which enables you to set up or plans that promote you payouts. Saving for rainy days can help you when times are choppy. Besides, you can take out life policies, or mortgage policies that offer money when times are rough. Consequently, the policies can provide you benefit to keep your home and/or car when you hit hard spots in your life.

New relationships can add strain, in which could advance to or depression. Relationships at the start often endure stressful situations for the first year. Therefore, when starting a new intimate relationship make sure you discover someone that will support and work with you when times are hard. Thus, relationships bring many rewards, since you have someone to share your life with, as well as a mate to help you when you feel depressed.

Divorces are a leading cause of depression. Breakups are not friendly, yet you can discover positive coming from divorces. For example, if you are in an abusive relationship whether it is bodily, mental, or verbal, coming out of the relationship can save your life and mental health. Staying in the new intimate relationship could only advance to calamity.

For the largest part, you endure stress, in which comes from your environment, thoughts, or body. Therefore, downheartedness is either emotional stricken or else chemical related. Bipolar symptoms often stem from emotional negative energies, as well as chemical imbalances.

If you sought help and disclosed you do not have physiological problems causing the depression, or mental illness, thus you have a state of mind to work through to manage and checkmate depression. If you have

A physiological illness, such as a chemical imbalance you will need medications, therapy, and ongoing therapy from your doctor to work through the depression. Those in a state of mind could encourage from learning more about emotions. Since emotions is the key element that backs or depression. In other words, heart inclinations or emotional responses are the single, the largest reason why a person feels depressed.

The climate may increase stress, since you are, swayed by influences. Changes in the weather, noise pollution, interpersonal requirements, crowds, and so forth are all stress related facets that could cause you to lose self-esteem and confidence in self. Therefore, if your environment is holding you down, you may want to consider. The change will give you a positive outlook in life. Life net is too short to stay marooned in one place. If you have lost-lose situation relating to stress and change, thus you need to harmonize, your conceptions while understanding your emotions, thus managing and conquering depression.

Hierarchy in to Self-Reliance and Constructive Change

Guide to Self-Reliance and Constructive Change – How Stress and Self-Esteem Affect Us

Self-esteem plays a major role in your life affecting your attitude and outlook either positively or negatively. If you have a low opinion of yourself, it can hinder you physically, emotionally, and spiritually. Stress can affect your level of self-esteem as well as your mood.

How negative self-esteems rob you of your enjoyment:

A negative self-esteem can affect many areas of your life. It can be the cause of stress, loneliness, depression, and a lack of quality relationships. If you have self-esteem issues, they can intensify stress-causing problems in your sleep. Proper rest is necessary to deal with things that naturally happen on a daily basis.

Maintaining a healthy self-esteem helps you stay happy and keep your stress level down. You must think positively to live your life in a positive way.

Self-esteem is what we think about ourselves. Find ways to make your life more enjoyable by thinking more positively about yourself. Analyze what you can do to make your life less stressful.

With the proper skills, you can learn to relieve the stress that consumes you. Stress is inevitable but it does not have to be debilitating with proper stress management skills. Practice ways of managing stress. Search for the stress relief methods that work for you. As you learn to control the stress in your life, you will begin to have a more positive attitude about yourself.

A better self-image will lead to relaxation. Many resources available will help you learn to think more positively. Check online or at your local library, bookstore, or video outlet.

One good relaxation technique is meditation. Relaxation is positive and helps to relieve stress while improving your self-esteem. There are many forms of meditation such as nature sounds, aromatherapies, relaxing music. Focus on the stimuli and allow your mind to wander to relaxing environments. In fact, if you purchase the natural sounds of at your dollar stores, you can use your

Window Media to enjoy biofeedback or neurofeedback solutions that guide you to relaxation and meditation. Just insert the disk. Windows Media should start up; otherwise, you can start up the program. Click on the Visual area once the music starts to enjoy audio/video capabilities. What a great tool to guide you to relaxation.

Closing yourself away from all the distractions of life is another great way to relax. Lie down flat and relax all your muscles. Think about how every inch of your body feels on the bed. Breathe slowly and think soothing thoughts. Plug in a natural melody CD and let the flows and ebbs of motion waters pass by you onto the rocks in a lovely gathering of land. Use the Rushing Rivers, the Elements and music to sweep over you while it builds you energy, revitalizing your soul.

Some of these CDs, such as the Rushing River collection give you motion and music that combines wind, keys and strings of compositions to guide you to relaxation. The purpose of self-reliance is leaning on you, but sometimes having special aids, such as natural sounds can speed up the process, helping you make constructive change.

As you get used to this ritual, you will look forward to doing it on a daily basis. You will begin to feel better about yourself as the stress level in your life decreases. You will find that all the aspects of your life will be more positive. Once the stress declines, you can enjoy a free mind. Free minds usually have no problem finding solutions to solve their problems. Take time to explore your options. Learn to accept change.

Acceptance of Change as to Self Reliance and Constructive Change

Change is a necessary facet of life. It is through change that we are able to grow, adjust, and fix problems as they arise. Changes transform us in such a way that they dictate the way we live life. Although it is often feared, change should be seen as a positive thing.

Sometimes, bad habits sprout from an unwillingness to accept change. Allowing these habits to take root in our lives usually leads bigger changes such as depression, physical ailments and possibly even death.

Unwillingness to accept change is a problem of epic proportions because it not only affects the person struggling with the changes, but everyone around as well. A negative mood can quickly influence the moods of everyone close by.

If you desire to have a long, happy, fruitful life you must be willing to go with the flow of the changes in your life. Life can flow harmonically if you welcome change with open arms. Problems are inevitable. You cannot run from them, hide from them, or avoid them. It is not how many problems you have or don't have that determine your quality of life, but rather how you react to them.

Because change has always had a negative connotation, people have always had a hard time dealing with it. To see change as an opportunity instead of a set back, we must change the way we think about it.

Maintain control of your emotions. Do not deny your emotions, but keep a tight leash on them. Don't let your emotions control you, but think with your head. When you are letting fear, pain, anger, anxiety, etc control your thoughts you will make faulty judgments and therefore make matters worse.

Your attitude about the change will have a direct impact on how you handle it. Do you see this change as a substitute for what you are used to or as an opportunity to grow and move to another level in your life? What good can come of this situation? Where can you go from here that will be a productive path for your life?

A common example is debt. Too many times, people think the changes that have to be made to remedy the financial burden are impossible because it will require major lifestyle changes, which scare them. However, a helpful tip may be just what you need to get the ball rolling towards debt reduction. There are many suggestions available on the internet or at the library that really wouldn't make a major impact on your lifestyle, but will bring peace of mind and eventually lower debt.

One good way to learn to adapt to change is by starting to make gradual changes in your life. Start with something small like a new hairstyle. Maybe try an exercise plan or a new diet. Make a commitment to yourself and journal your progress. At the end of the first week, you will see a significant shift in the way you think about change (and you'll probably feel better physically, also).

You could change your lifestyle by changing one of your rituals. Instead of turning on the TV when you first come home, try picking up the phone and calling a friend, going to hang out, hop on the treadmill, or read a good book.

As you try new things and make minor changes in your life, you'll be much more confident when the inevitable changes come your way. You will also notice a brighter outlook on life and you might even be healthier.

What you think dictates your actions. As you make positive changes in your thought process, you will notice that your actions will be more positive as well. Get your guide to search the soul.

Guide to Self Reliance and Constructive Change through Soul Searching

Soul searching is one way to bring about constructive changes in your life as you find and the tools within yourself to rely upon. Sometimes it's difficult to break through those behaviors we all learn as children, but it's not impossible.

It may take some will power to discover your inner strengths and manage the changes that need to be made. There are many resources online to help you find who you really are.   Making constructive changes and discovering independency are not beyond your grasp.

All that you need to accomplish your goals is inside of you. Take the time necessary to search for stability within yourself and analyze what you need to do to stand on your own. Ask for help and encouragement. There are many helpful guides available to assist you in finding practices that are most therapeutic for you. Be creative in inventing your guide to success.

There are many new ideas you can use to find the self-dependency you are striving for. You know yourself better than they know anyone and using your inner guide to direct you will lead you to strengths that will help you find these new ideas. As you search yourself, you will find the resources you already possess.

Relying only on yourself, you will find your world is unique to you. You will find who you are as an individual, your own autonomy, the direction to take control of your own life.

Don't expect the changes to happen over night, but don't give up. If you continue to press on towards the goals you have set for yourself you will see the negative things in you life begin to change. You have to change the way you think as you tap into the resources and skills you found.

As the changes become apparent, you will find yourself gradually becoming more in control of your life. Your attitude about things will completely turn around and you'll find you have a more optimistic personality.

You will discover there is more to life than sitting around watching television or doing other unproductive things. You will desire to spend more quality time on activities that will make a difference in the end. Other negative behaviors and habits won't be so appealing anymore. You won't want to engage in the things that used to bring you down because you will be able to see the negative effect these things really have.

Indulge yourself. Begin to seek out self-reliance and constructive thinking guides online. Just thinking about it is sparking the desire to change, isn't it? You're looking forward to making changes in your life to improve yourself.

Others will see the changes also. Your hard work is going to show and others are going to want to know how you did it so they can do it too. Then you will have a started a new positive thinking trend among your peers.

However, move slowly so that the changes last. If you find yourself slipping backwards, step back and look at some of the other ideas you came up with. Variety will ensure success. If you try to hurry though, you will only hinder your progress. Any major changes that are going last requires a process that must be followed and skipping steps or rushing through steps will negate the work you've done.

Set up small goals within the larger goal to guarantee permanent changes. If you fall, don't beat yourself up as that only ensures failure. Pick yourself up, dust yourself off, and keep going as if you never fell. Look back only to see the progress you've made ignoring those few times you tripped. Keep pressing on and you will succeed!

Go on the hunt for your guide to self-reliance to make positive changes.

In Hunt of to Self Reliance and Constructive Change

Look out to sea. Imagine seeing a ship in the distance with its wings up and all of a sudden for no apparent reason the ship starts to sink. Slowly, the ship lowers its bow into the water with the stern raising to give it a push so that it sinks deeper.

Picture it. Like this action-taking place, we as people are out to sea. Some of us pay attention so we don't lose control, yet others carelessly sail along. In route they may have success along the way, but as time goes on because they did not bother to plan or make decisions that would determine their faith, someone in that ocean oh Betsy is going to drown.

Inquiring Mind is one way to bring about constructive changes in your life as you discover and the tools within yourself to depend upon. Sometimes it's backbreaking to break through those behaviors we all learned as children, but it's not impractical.

It may take some will dynamism to discover your constitutional deepest courage and manage the changes that compulsions to be made. There are many resources online to guide me to you find who you really are. Commanding constructive changes and discovering independency are not beyond your grasp.

Take the time compelling to search for dependable within yourself and analyze what you need to do to stand on your own feet. Ask for support but never expect anything from another person, rather just accept encouragement when it comes your way. There are many helpful guides attainable to assist you in finding practices that are most therapeutic for you. Be formative in creative your guide to achievement.

Dependency you are striving for. You know yourself better than they know anyone and using your inner guide to direct you will lead you to strengths that will help you discover these new ideas. As you search yourself, you will find the reserves you already possess.

Relying only on yourself, you will find your world is unique to you. You will discover who you are as a person, your own self-rule or liberty, and the direction to take control of your own life net. Many new ideas you can use to find the Self-dependency you are climbing for. You know yourself better more so they know anyone and using your inner guide to direct you could lead you to strengths that could help you find these new ideas. As you search yourself, you will find the reserves you already possess.

Depending only on you, you will discover your universe in a different light. You might discover who you are, which amounts to a heap of beans when you are soul searching.

Once you see the way to make constructive changes, you will not be someone out at sea in wonderment as to what to expect next. Sometimes you have to set plans, make decisions, etc. It is all a part of life.

Once last time, peer out in the ocean. Visualize a ship in the distance with its wings flapping along and suddenly for no apparent explanation, the ship begins to sink. Slowly, the ship's bow lowers into the cold waters with the stern lifting in the air to give the bow a shove so that it starts to sink deeper.

Now put you on that ship and ask...Did I plan for this occasion. Am I prepared to handle dangers or risks that come my way? While this may not mean anything to you, the point is sometimes life is full of risks and it is a chance you have to take. The chance you may take involves self-reliance and constructive changes also.

Discovering Resources, Guide to Self-Reliance and Constructive Changes

It is fairly simple to find resources in your quest to make positive changes in your life. The hardest part is uncovering the source of your angst. Once you have done that, success is just around the corner.

You could begin by assessing who you are, what you like and don't like about yourself, what makes you tick. Look at your emotional make up. As you seek deep within yourself you will begin to see what changes need to take place. Only you can make those changes, so you are the only one who can determine which methods will work.

Find external resources as well. The self-help section of your library or local bookstore is overflowing with materials that will help you on your endeavor. There is a vast majority of information on the internet about meditation techniques, ways to change your thought patterns, and support groups and forums to help you change bad habits.

Setting goals is a great way to get started. Don't go for the "gusto goals" that seem unobtainable. Start with a small goal. For instance, if you eat nothing but fast food and you want to change you are eating habits; don't start shopping at Wild Oats Market. Start by adding a serving of vegetables a day, or cutting back on grease one meal a day. The effects of minor changes will encourage you to take the next step. Before you know it, Wild Oats will be your grocery store of choice.

Write your goals down and keep up with your progress on paper. Make a chart on a poster board and hang it in your bedroom. It will help you to visualize the goal and the victory. The smaller the goals, the more victories you will have to record. As you look at the list of victories you will be encouraged to set another goal and achieve it.

Emotional stress is exhausting. When you control your emotions, you will have more energy for more productive activities. Relaxation is a great way to corral the energy you would be wasting on stress. Notice your surroundings. Listen to birds or soft music to get your focus off your problems. Once you relax, begin to release that energy by getting up and doing something constructive – clean house, exercise, go for a walk.

Meditation is a wonderful way to control your thoughts. Stress makes your mind go in fifty directions at once, but focusing on one thing at a time will help, you calm down. You will begin to feel more energetic because stress is very taxing on your energy level. You will also make better decisions because you will think them through first.

Exercise is a great way to expel the newfound energy. Not to mention the fact that it is a healthy habit to get into. Stress causes high blood pressure while exercise strengthens your heart. Stress causes disrupted sleep while exercise leads to a night full of rest. The best part of exercise is that it's free. All you have to do is walk out the front door and around the block.

As you begin to dictate your life as opposed to your circumstances dictating you, you will begin to notice positive changes naturally taking place. You will notice others around you begin to relax and life will flow much more easily.

You have already taken the first step by reading this article. Take the next step to a better you today. Once you get past the first step, the rest will follow. The main point is, never give up hope.

Self-Reflection, to Self-Reliance and Constructive Change

There are moments in your life when you will just

stop, take a look at your life and realize that you aren't where you want to be. Your life is out of control, or perhaps too in control, at any rate... you're not happy. This moment of internal thought, this self-reflection, this is your first step towards making a constructive and meaningful change in your life.

You have just realized that you're not achieving your full potential or that you're stuck in a job you hate. While this may seem like a dismal and depressing realization, it is a blessing in disguise. You are well on your way to improving your life. Armed with this motivation, you now have set the foundation for a better you.

There are amazing guides and tools available online to help you on your quest to improve yourself. If you know you're not making the most of your life and you want to be all that you can be, there is a way.

The first step is done, you have personally identified a problem and you are now striving to fix it. This is the first step towards your self-reliance and your new life. Because you are your own source of motivation for change, it will be that much easier to bring about change. Because you are helping yourself, you are becoming more self-reliant with every constructive change you make.

Although you may think that this battle is fierce, tiring and sometimes even hopeless... you don't have to do this alone. You will encounter many inspirations and examples in everyday life that will propel you from a simple want to a fiery passion.

Placid lakes, amazingly bright blue skies, a crisp walk on an autumn day. While seemingly ordinary and dull, these beautiful and natural experiences are just one example of the small things in life that you'll come to appreciate and draw inspiration from. So take some time to yourself, take a relaxing walk; be alone with your thoughts. It is only from doing this that you will uncover not only the problems but the solutions.

Armed with this new and unique perspective, there is nothing that you can't achieve. This state of mind will let you dive into the depths of your psyche, uncover the major conflicts and problems that have haunted you and inhibited your way to success and give you the power to solve them on your own.

The problem with depending on others for problem solving is that you don't grow as a person. It's simply a band-aid remedy for a much bigger wound. Your life is hurt, your mind and your thoughts are injured and you need to perform a surgery. If you cannot learn to rely on yourself and solve these problems in your own ways than you will always have problems that haunt you.

Becoming self-reliant is the one change you will make in your life that you will never regret. As time passes and you experience more, you will never find a time where you wish you weren't so self-reliant. This is because you will never let yourself down. You are in control of yourself, so why would you knowingly sabotage your own health? That's right, you wouldn't. You know exactly what you need, so why trust anyone else with your life.

These changes will not come instantly; it will take hard work and dedication to bring about the changes you want in your life. Realizing you have problems, however, is the first step towards making these changes. Without this step, you will be stuck on the bottom rung, letting life pass you by and letting every opportunity slip away. You think you're overweight. You want to lose weight. Take some initiative! Take a walk, admire the nature around you, find something you love and use that inspiration to make change. It might take months; it might take years, but if you trust in yourself than you can always achieve your goals.

Constructive changes to Self-Reliance and Constructive Change Through Meditation

Sometimes you need to just take a moment to relax, to appreciate the world around you, to get in tune with your inner-self... a moment to just be you. Meditation can give you this moment. Not a gimmick or a scheme, not a quick fix or a shady deal, meditation is an age-old tradition passed down through cultures and celebrated throughout time.

Meditation clears your mind and allows for the free passage of spiritual ideas and prophetic thoughts. While meditation may seem like nothing more than a way to kill time or a quirky fad, it can lead you to a better life.

The thing most inhibiting the changes people need in their lives is stress. We are too stressed about our jobs, our relationships, and our T.V. shows...heck, even our pets! We obsess and stress over every teeny-tiny and minute thing until it drives us crazy. With all this stress, it's a wonder why nothing ever goes the way we want it.

You want those new pair of loafers, but you're so stressed about paying bills and keeping your wife happy that you don't even take the time to figure out a way that you could save the money for them. You want to take a trip to Athens... too bad your boss is breathing down your neck about that proposal he wants on his desk by Monday! Don't you ever wish you could just look inside yourself, take the time to figure it all out and just do it? Well you can, with meditation. There are tons of tools and guides online to help you achieve your goals through meditation.

It's not hard, starting with a small, five-minute session each day and gradually increasing your time as needed. All it takes is for you to set aside 30 minutes to an hour each day for you. As busy as your life is, I'm sure you can spare that. Now what you need to do is just relax. Think of what it would be like to be happy; to have your most desired feelings met. Now clear your mind. Take in the world around you, absorbing it all and channeling the feeling and spirit from everything. Cleanse your mind by removing all your negative and impure thoughts and just relaxing, being peaceful.

With a clear mind and a focused intellect, you can now set your sharply honed skills on the problems in your life. Now you have a period of time during the day where you can relax, be yourself and tackle those things you want to change but never had the time. Those shoes you wanted. What about that bonus you're getting at the end of the month.
How about a hat trip to Athens, Well couldn't you schedule a meeting with the president of the Athens' facility of your company?

When you take the time to sit down, relax, and clear your mind, you are able to depend on yourself to get vital things done. Instead of relying on blackberries, pagers and laptops in this hectic world just think basic. All you need is your mind and some time alone. With these two tools, you'll be able to rely on just yourself to solve any task that may be troubling you. Even major life decisions will become easier to make when you're focused and relaxed.

The first step to improving your life is to improve the trust you have in yourself, only then will the rest follow. Taking the time to clear your head, enjoy life and just let yourself feel relaxed is the best strategy you could ever follow. It will not only improve the quality of your thought, but the reliability of yourself as well.

**Think Positively! to Self-Reliance and
Constructive Change**

Without positive thought, there is no room for constructive change and self-reliance to blossom and develop. By training ourselves to think positively and enthusiastically, we can delve inside our minds and uncover the strengths that even we didn't know we had inside of ourselves. Thinking positive is the only surefire way to bring about change in your life and to start you on the road to self-reliance and constructive changes in your life.

Trust your subconscious. Sometime during the day, stop yourself and just look at the situation around you. Are you happy? Do you feel like this is where you want to be? Do you feel at home, comfortable or content with the situation? Most importantly, do you feel like the career or job that you're in is something you can continue doing?

If you realize you're not happy with your job or your career, it's time to figure out why. When you walk by a shiny window or a full-length mirror, do you look at yourself? Do you like how you look or do you cringe at the sight of who you are? If you are disgusted with what you have become, there's no need in lamenting and being depressed. This realization is your first step towards happiness.

Think positively. Instead of thinking about all of the things in your life that are going wrong, come up with ideas and situations that could make you happy. Dream up the perfect job or the perfect relationship, and then strive to find it! When you're thinking positively and enthusiastically, you are more likely to be energetic and outgoing and thus are more likely to make better connections both business wise and relationship wise.

By using this positive thought, you are now thinking for yourself. You are using the good thoughts and ideas that dwell inside of you to bring about change. This is self-reliance. You are relying on the thoughts and ideas that you, yourself, have come up with by thinking positively to bring about the changes you want. These constructive changes are what you are striving to achieve.

Before you go about making your constructive changes, you must ask yourself "Is this what I really want?" Because if you're trying to make changes in your life that you're not completely happy with, you'll soon find yourself back at square one. In order to achieve happiness, you have to want the changes you're bringing about.

If your job is too stressful, use your positive thought to get a promotion. If the promotion that you get doesn't improve your happiness or your comfort, maybe you should think about switching careers. If the very nature or idea of your job gets you down, than maybe you're not cut out for that field of work. Use your positive thoughts to find out what you're good at and then do it!

There is no situation in your life that cannot be improved. If you think that, your life is hopeless, going nowhere, dead end, than you're probably right. If you believe that you can change that and that you can eventually be happy with your job and personal life, then you will be.

The key to any situation is not to let your negative thoughts weigh you down. When you think negatively, you doubt yourself. Self-doubt makes you less likely to trust your instincts and the concept of self-reliance is thrown straight out the window. In order to bring about constructive change in your life through self-reliance, you must do just what the strategy implies and rely on yourself! If you think positively, have hope and trust in your potential, you will achieve great things.

Less Stress, Less Mess: to Self-Reliance and Constructive Change

Stress is the major cause of unhappiness among the population today. When you're stressed, you are bogged down with negative thoughts, feelings and ideas. Remove the stress from your life and watch the happiness, good thoughts and comfort roll back into your life. Removing stress will vastly increase your state of health; help you to live longer and actually enjoy the longer life you'll be living. Fear, unhappiness, anger, frustration, and sadness... these things can all lead to a very stressed-out life. Being stressed can have you feeling threatened, frightened and scared of change. With people of the modern era working twice as long, twice as hard, and for half the incentive, it's no wonder the population is so stressed! All this stress leads to frequent illness and can even result in death!

Stress isn't entirely evil, however. Although this might seem radical, funny and even absurd, stress can be one of the greatest motivators you can have!

Above everything else, you must not fret about your current situation. Even if your lot in life is not nearly what you expected, you have no idea what the future holds, so why be glum? You need to slow down your life and live it day-by-day, if not second by second, so you can maximize the amount of effort and time put into your life. If you are experiencing tension constantly, you may want to look into therapeutic ways to relieve this tension such as massages, herbal teas or nice relaxing walks. Turning to things like drugs or alcohol for release is a bad idea and will only set you back in progress. If for instance, you aren't getting enough sleep and you think that alcohol with calm you and let you get the rest you need, you are wrong. Alcohol interrupts the essential REM sleep your body needs and can mess up your entire internal clock system.

Instead, you can make a trip to the local pharmacy and make a purchase of some herbal supplements to help you relax and sleep. These supplements will relax your nerves and provide you with a comfortable, REM-filled sleep. These supplements will cost much less than narcotics or alcohol and will be much safer and healthier for your system, contributing even more to your overall removal of stress. The problem with most people is that they are unable to detect stress when they are actually having it, most people will have many signs of a stressful life and not even know it!

The classic sign of stress is when you are overly irritable. When you are constantly on the edge, very sensitive, judgmental or quick-tempered you are most likely over-worked and over-stressed. Pessimistic attitudes are quick to take offence or otherwise very emotional are also signs that you are stressed, which you will need to control. Bodily signs like twitching, nail biting and sweating are very good indicators of stress, as well as more serious and threatening signs like nausea, ulcers and excessive consumption of cigarettes or alcohol. When you find it almost impossible to focus or concentrate on one thing, it's most likely that your mind is swimming with too many thoughts.

Moreover, you are overworked because of stress. Obsessing over decisions, being incredibly meticulous about meaningless things and being too analytical or a "perfectionist" may also be warning signs of stress. Various emotional symptoms that indicate stress can be, low self-esteem, panic attacks, uncontrollable anger, jealousy, constantly being on the verge of tears, bad dreams, uncontrollable laughter or even the inability to laugh.

All of this stress is incredibly detrimental to both your health and your state in life. By realizing that stress could very well be your main problem, this could motivate you to rid your life of stress and therefore increase your happiness exponentially.

Enjoying Life to Improve Your Life: to Self-Reliance and Constructive Change

Our lives are very heavily dependant on self-esteem and feeling good about what we do. If we're feeling unhappy, stressed or depressed about whom we are and what we're doing, it lowers our potential and can even contribute to illness. Stress is an especially troublesome factor in determining how happy we are in life. That barrier of stress erected between you and your goal, it will seem almost impossible to penetrate. Self-esteem is extremely important to establishing a happy and balanced life. If we're at peace with our selves and the stress in our lives is down than we will be, happier and healthier and good things will start to come to us.

Negative thoughts and bad self-image will contribute to massive stress, negative work environments and bad relationships. There are so many negative aspects of our life that we dwell on and that make us unhappy. We feel trapped and controlled by these negative things, but in reality we have the power to conquer them.

The power to control these negative thoughts and turn them into positive thinking lies in doing things for you. Taking a day to just relax and do the things you, love can drastically improve your situation. Just watch some television, catch up on your reading, take a nice refreshing walk... you'll feel better about yourself for doing all of the things you love. Because you're happy, about whom you are and what you're doing, other positive things will follow.

We need things like this, little getaways from reality in which we can indulge our needs, to improve our happiness and positive thoughts. Positive thought is the best motivator that you can have, it reduces stress and makes you rely more on who you are as a person and not on the things, you have access to. This is not a quick fix for depression or an instant get-rich-quick scheme, this is hard and life changing work.

Self-esteem is how we perceive ourselves; it is the opinion we hold towards who we are as people. If you are letting stress, take over your life, your self-esteem is going to be extremely low and you'll feel helpless all the time. Think about what changes you can make in your life to relieve some of that stress you're feeling. Think about what you can do for yourself that will make life more enjoyable. Make these changes in your life and you will no doubt see a change in your mood and your experiences.

It's takes hard work and dedication to be able to relax in our lives and to relieve ourselves of stress, but it can be done, and once it is you will feel terrific. Getting rid of all of our stress is not realistic, there will always be unexpected things that come up and stress us out. However, getting rid of all the stress that doesn't need to be there is perfectly doable. A good way to do this is through music. Find a band, genre or song that you love and just take five or ten minutes a day to just sit or lay there, listening to the music and relaxing. Clear you mind, interpret the song, picture the lyrics, do whatever you feel, but just take the time to sit yourself down and relax. This seemingly simple thing is the key to your personal happiness.

Because you want change in your life, constructive change, you're striving to love yourself. If you love who you are you'll be able to put more trust in what you're capable of doing. By doing this, you've set the ball in motion. You now trust yourself to make change.

Fear of Change to Self Reliance and Constructive Change

The main deciding factor, the thing that can mould and shape our lives the way we please, the one thing that can set in motion the conveyor belt that is our lives is... change. While seemingly a simple concept, many people overlook the fact that to achieve the constructive changes you want in life; you must first accept the fact that your life will be different. Fear of change is extremely common in most people, even people who are unhappy with their lives fear change. Change can be hurtful, but only if you prevent it from happening. Because then, you become stuck, your life deteriorates and you spiral quickly into unhappiness.

This unhappiness often manifests itself in the form of illegal activities such as drugs or prostitution, activities that have adverse affects on your health such as smoking or alcohol abuse or even unethical behavior such as promiscuity or adultery. These habits all have two things in common... they're an impractical solution to a growing problem, and they lead only to more unhappiness.

People who can't learn to accept changes in their lives will continue to run on the treadmill of unhappiness until they die. Why just accept that you're not fond of your life, why not just does something about it? Too afraid that the change will disrupt the daily routine you've come to despise anyway. There's no reason to fear change because change is the essence of all that can be good.

So of course, you want to live healthier and longer, you want to be happier, more cheerful and less angry. The problem is that you want it quick and easy without effort or change. Unfortunately, you're going to have to face obstacles on this path to greatness. These obstacles and problems you face is just the natural order of things. In order to bring about great changes, you must first conquer great obstacles. Some say the journey is its own reward; other saner people, however, say that the reward is only obtained if there *is* a journey.

The main reason why people cannot accept change is that they fail to understand the nature of change. Many people still keep strong the beliefs of their ancestors. Change is disruptive, anarchistic and wrong. However, this is simply not the case; change is merely a logical progression of things. Change is the channeling of positive energy to bring about positive changes. If you take all of your positive and hopeful thoughts about owning a new washer and dryer and put them to use to motivate you into getting a promotion or a bonus at work, you have achieved change.

The best change you can make in your life is one of a lifestyle change. Whether it is diet, exercise or otherwise, a positive lifestyle choice will almost always contribute to a positive life. You can start with a 30-minute walk daily. Not too far, maybe to the corner store for some milk, around the block and home, you'll feel good about yourself because you, yourself, have made change. You have stocked up on milk and you've exercised. Not only have you done a household chore, but also you've become healthier along the way!

What most people don't know is that the thoughts that occur in your mind are soon manifested in your habits and behaviors. If you are surrounded by violent and criminal behavior or crude and repulsive acts, you will begin to exude these tendencies and commit these acts. If you watch television shows laced with nudity, violence and excessive cursing, it will present itself in your mannerisms and dialogue.

While there are many ways to let change take over your life, provide you with an extremely negative outcome, if you just keep thinking positive, and think of change and a welcome thing in your home, you'll be on your way to success sooner than you think.

Realizing Your Potential in   to Self Reliance and Constructive Change

It can take only a moment for you to realize just who you are and just what you're able to do, and at this moment you can harness these feelings for constructive changes in your life. We can all make constructive changes in our lives, even those of us who are completely set in our ways, afraid of change or feel that since that's the way they were brought up, they can't change. You're wrong, you can change and you can be happy.

If you want to work towards making things in your life happen for you, it is possible and you can do it. Don't get discouraged because the task seems daunting, it's more than doable when you realize you're potential. You just need to be able to set aside some time each day to reflect on your life and yourself and to use those ideas and feelings to motivate you!

We are all able to make constructive changes, even if we feel like we're hopeless. If you have enough will power, the realization you want to change, and a positive outlook... the rest will follow suit shortly. You never have to go it alone, however, there are many beautiful and helpful guides and tricks to help you along the way, and all you have to do is seek them out. While these guides and tricks may help you along, you can't rely on them to do the work for you. Truly to be happy, the work must come from within you.

Depending on"you" opens up a world of possibilities for growth and change. You will suddenly find yourself doing all the things you've always dreamt of and loving it. With a fierce determination and a realization of what you know your potential is... just what you COULD be doing, there's nothing stopping you.

Relying on yourself is the most critical skill you will ever learn. Through the process of realizing what you can be, you will begin to see that yourself more positively. This new positive self-image will make you feel much better about trusting in yourself and your instincts. Although constructive changes will most likely take time, this is no reason to get discouraged. With this positive reinforcement, you can change anything in your life you feel you should, whether it be losing weight or switching jobs. These changes will help you regain control of your life and stop living by what the world wants you to. This guide is to help you become the best you that there is.

Constructive changes are essential to the improvement of your life. Changing your old and detrimental habits for new and healthy ones or simply just making smart lifestyle choices will make you feel much better about your situation in life. Changing your lazy and lethargic ways, such as being a couch potato all day, to more productive things like taking a walk can all be done if you just realize you have the potential to change.

You will begin to look forward to life and to living it when you begin to make changes for the better. Your outlook will brighten up your life and even the lives of those around you. When positive changes are made in your life, this is exuded through your cheerful disposition and co-workers or bosses may notice and make good comments, leading to more success! Don't forget being positive and happy is setting a good example for everyone else too; this will result in happier work and social environments.

This isn't one huge struggle however; sometimes you must let your hair down and give yourself a reward for your hard work. Just reflect on all the progress you have made and celebrate it by buying yourself something nice, going out with the people, asking that girl at the coffee house on a date. Reward yourself for taking initiative by taking some initiative!

From Relaxation to Self Reliance and Constructive Change

Relaxation is by far the one thing that the people of today overlook. Most people are too busy or stressed to take time and relax. Little do they know that this inability to just stop, clear your head and be self-analytical is what's bringing about the negativity in their lives? By relaxing, we can learn to explore the wonders and possibilities of our minds. We can find new and interesting ideas we didn't know we had and we can put them to good use in improving our lives. Relaxation is what can start you on your path to making constructive changes in you life and relying more on yourself and less on others.

Relying on other people and even computer programs may seem like a quick and effective way to unload your problems but in reality, it's doing you more harm than good. By doing this, you are constantly avoiding the responsibilities and problems that you face in your life. If you are face-to-face with a problem you can't outsource, a problem that a computer can't fix, will you be prepared? Shirking all of your problems and responsibilities onto other people inhibits your ability to grow and learn as a person. As a result, you will be most likely stuck in a dead-end job that you hate, surrounded by people who you despise.

Are you happy with who you are and what you do? If not, ask yourself why not. If you aren't happy with yourself, chances are this has a very negative impact on your life. There are many things you can do to improve your self-esteem and the way you see yourself. Take five minutes to write down on paper all of the things about yourself that you feel are unique or that you feel proud of. Now do the same with all of the things you feel are negative about you or bringing you down. Now take the list of negative things and burn it. You should then proceed to hang the list of positive things somewhere in your house where you will see it every day. This will remind you of what a good person you can be and how much you are important.

Relaxation doesn't necessarily mean having no problems; this is why people are unable to relax. People believe that in order to relax, their life has to be rid of anything that is problematic or stressful. While this would be ideal, it's simply not possible. This why people never get the results they want by unloading their problems on others and manifesting their stress into terrible habits.

What you need to do is to take time to yourself each day. It doesn't have to be much, maybe only an hour. Use this time to do something that is cathartic, something that takes your frustrations and problems and channels them into something positive and relaxing. Take up jogging or boxing, start writing a novel; maybe even start a little business for you. The point is that you should be doing something that is fun for you and that you love.

Once you start relaxing and not constantly worrying about the problems in your life, solutions to these problems will emerge. You will begin to think clearer and you mind will not be so crowded with negative thoughts. This will allow the emergence and free passage of positive thoughts and interesting ideas. You can now harness this power to bring about positive and constructive changes in your life.

When you use this new clear head to concentrate, analytically, on the situation and just figure out what needs to be done, the solutions will flow through you like rain. This guide to self-reliance and constructive changes may seem simple, but that's only because it is. If you take the time to slow life down, you will begin to see things much clearer.

Hobbies as to Self Reliance and Constructive Change

Our lives can be so filled with stress; hectic running

around and constant worrying ensure we don't have time to enjoy the things we love. Because of this, our creativity and potential are stifled heavily. We don't realize just how much more we can achieve because we don't give ourselves a chance to channel all of our thoughts and ideas. Therefore, instead of inventing a cure for a disease, we're simply working 9 to 5 in a dead end job. Do you want to be able to realize your full potential and to channel it into something good? Well if you want to be able to make change in your life, you need to start by doing something very simple: Take up a hobby!

You may think of this as being silly, even ludicrous advice, but in reality, it's going to be the major driving force in your life. In a hectic, workaday world we live in now, we hardly give ourselves time to breathe, let alone have a hobby. Because of this, all of our free flowing ideas and creativity instead manifest themselves into frustration, jealousy and anger. These negative thoughts consume us. In addition, will ultimately be our downfall.

Start by taking thirty minutes a day to yourself. Even if this seems like it will interrupt the time you need to work or to stress out about your life, it's worth it in the end. The changes you bring about will far outweigh the minute possibility of it having a negative impact.

This is the first step, and you've done it. You've set aside time each day for you to channel your ideas and creativity into something productive. Whether it is building your stamp collection, learning to play guitar, writing a novel or simply just taking a walk, do it. The things you love to do are being done. This will make you feel better about the kind of person you are. You will begin to like who you are much more than you did. Because your ideas and thoughts now have an outlet, they won't build up and put pressure on you. By taking thirty minutes a day to yourself to do something fun, you have just removed a major source of stress in your life.

While seemingly simple, this process has started you on the way to a happier and healthier life. With a reduced amount of stress, you reduce your risk of illnesses like the flu, colds, ulcers and even death. Your negative stress has now been replaced with positive potential.

Starry nights, glorious sunsets, crisp summer evenings, will all start to present themselves as beautiful and interesting works of art. While they used to seem ordinary and natural, you will now see them as sources of inspiration and power.

You will begin to derive satisfaction from the experience of seeing a sunset. You might even channel your feelings into that new song you're writing. Maybe that new song you just wrote will be good enough to get some radio play. The possibilities are endless.

You will be able to achieve everything you desire with this new and improved outlook on life. This process will let you discover your positive thoughts and ideas and use them to replace the negativity and stress that plagues you. All of the worries and problems in your life you can also channel into your hobby. Use your anger as a motivation to write an inspired poem. Use the hostile relationship with a co-worker as the basis for a short story.

Although seemingly simple, these changes will not come quickly without effort. Taking the time to do what you love and to start a hobby is the most important step. You have set the stage for becoming a better person and improving your life. Thinking positive will bring you rewards.

Positive Thinking is the Key to Self Reliance and Constructive Change

what do you see when you look in the mirror? Are you happy with your appearance? How do you feel about your career? Do you take some responsibility for your own fate? Alternatively, do you feel that you are a victim of circumstance? Are your general thoughts and feelings about yourself and your life more positive than negative?

If your reaction to taking a good look at yourself in the mirror is not positive, you have some work to do before you are on the path to self-reliance and constructive change in your life. You have to be comfortable with who you are before you can develop a positive outlook and a sense of control over your destiny.

Positive thinking is a powerful tool for self-reliance and constructive change. For many people, positive thinking is the key to unlocking long-term happiness and satisfaction. In order to experience constructive change in life, you must develop the self-reliance that comes as a result of positive thinking.

Positive thinking is necessary to incorporate constructive changes in ones life. Fully to enjoy the benefits of self-reliance, positive thinking is necessary. Positive thinking is strongly linked to self-awareness. Through positive thoughts people are able to discover who they are at the core, and find their inner selves and hidden strengths.

Positive thinking will helps us make changes necessary for lifelong success and happiness, and guides us in the right direction toward having a positive outlook on life. Great deals of the attitudes we develop toward life develop subliminally, which means that we do not consciously decide to have the attitudes that we have. The way that we think and view the world affects our overall attitude. Negative thinking leads to a negative outlook. Positive thinking influences the development of positive emotions and reactions to feelings. This is how positive thinking can lead to constructive change.

When you train yourself to think positive thoughts, your outlook will improve. You will be able to base the decisions you make from a positive foundation. When you think positive, you become more self reliant, and take ownership of your responsibility for your own happiness and self-reliance.

If your career is a challenging area for you, the first decision that you need to make is whether or not you are in the right career. If so, ask yourself how you can change your negative feelings about your career into positive feelings, so that you will have an opportunity to be successful.

Conversely, if you realize that, you are not in the right career or workplace; focus on identifying what it is about your current situation that is not right for you. Once you know what you don't look, seek career opportunities in a field or environment that will be a better fit for you. If you choose to stay in the wrong environment, then you are choosing to allow negativity to remain in your life. Take responsibility for your own happiness, and take positive steps toward finding the career that is best for you and your long-term positive energy.

No one but you can answer the question about whether or not your current career is right for you. When you realize that your happiness is in your own hands and you take positive steps to improve your situation, you will enjoy the benefits of the self-reliance and constructive change that can evolve from positive thinking and proactive actions.

Many people find meditation to be very helpful when faced with making an important change. Change can be frightening, but positive change is sometimes a necessary step for managing stress and taking control of your destiny. Meditation can be a powerful tool for enhancing your self-reliance and positive thinking skills. Take a vacation from stress.

Self Reliance Can Help You Take A Vacation from Stress

How doe you see life?   Do you view life as an enjoyable vacation adventure?   Are you open to change? Are you prepared to take a few detours? Alternatively, do you have to follow a set path dictated by people and circumstances beyond your control?   Do you allow yourself to become and remain miserable by fretting and worrying over things that you can't control?

The way you look at life has a major impact on the stress you experience in your day-to-day life.   By viewing life as a pleasant vacation with yourself in the driver's seat, you can greatly reduce the anxiety, stress, and overall negativity in your life.

Where does stress come from?   Stress is a response to emotions. You have the ability to be in control of both the emotions you experience and how you respond to them. Whose responsibility is it to reduce the stress in your life? It is yours! You must take control of your emotions and manage the stress that can have a negative impact on your day-to-day life.

There is absolutely no point in fretting about things that you can't control. It is within your power to make a conscious decision to take control of your life and focus your energy on the positive, controllable aspects of your life. You have to deal with situations as they arise so that you can move on. Avoidance is negative, whether you are avoiding doing a task that you don't want to do or you are avoiding making a decision. Self-reliant, positive people experience less stress than others because they deal with life as it happens. They don't avoid things that need to be handled.

In order to make constructive changes in your life, you must first build your self-esteem.
You have to make a decision to take responsibility for living your life in a positive manner. You have to realize that you are the boss of yourself, and act accordingly. Everyone can implement constructive change in his or her life. Becoming independent is

within your reach.

To build the self-esteem that you need to become self reliant, take the time to search within yourself and discover what aspects of how you think and live need to be changed before you can stand on your own two feet. By banishing negative thoughts of avoidance and self-doubt from your mind, you can change your life for the better.

Whether you realize it or not, you know more than other people do about what is best for you. By listening to your inner self, you will find the strength to do what you need to do to bring about positive changes in your life. You will probably discover depths of strength that you never knew you had.

You don't have completely to cut yourself off from other people. It is take support and from positive people in your life when it is offered, but you must not put yourself in a position of depending on other people for your own happiness.

Through self-reliance, you will see the world through fresh eyes, and will be more open to the positive possibilities that area available to you.

Making plans is an important part of long-term success in life. Wouldn't you rather make plans for a positive journey than a long, uphill climb? By developing the ability to rely on yourself, you will arm yourself with the ability to cope with the challenges that come your way. You have no better ammunition than to arm yourself with the ability to rely on you.

Willpower in Self Reliance and Constructive Change

Sit down and think about where you can find your willpower to make constructive changes. You are the only one who can change your own behavior. Changing any type of habitual, negative behavior requires willpower. When you want to change your behavior, the first thing that you have to do is make a conscious decision to change. Once you make a decision to change, you have then stuck to that decision. The ability to follow through with a change you have decided to make is what willpower is all about.

Willpower requires a conscious effort to put mind over matter. When you want or crave something that you know is bad for you, it takes will power to avoid giving in to temptation. Willpower is an important component of self-reliance. You have consciously to stay away from negative or harmful activities through an act of will in order to change your behavior long term.

You are the only person who can change your own behavior. Once you make a decision to change, you will have an easier time sticking to your decision if you come up with a set of strategies designed to keep you from losing your willpower.

Many times, the secrets to changing your behavior lie in your subconscious mind. By reflecting internally, you may be able to discover solutions to behavior change that are buried within your subconscious. You may also want to do some external research of willpower and behavior change. There are many books and Internet resources that provide this type of information. However, simply becoming aware of barriers to change or the secrets of how to change isn't enough to bring about change. You have to make a decision and take action to bring about change on your won.

Many people want to give up smoking. Quitting smoking is a very difficult thing to do. However, there are many reasons to give up smoking. Smoking is an expensive, unhealthy, and unattractive habit. Very few people who smoke want to keep smoking, but they are not successful when they attempt to give up the habit.

Those who are not successful at their attempts to quit smoking frequently say that they didn't have the willpower to break the addiction to nicotine. Instead of being self-reliant enough to have the willpower to accomplish their goals, they give in to cravings. Other people are successful at giving up smoking. Many of those who are successful use strategies that can help them improve their will power. For example, some people engage in activities designed to keep their mouths busy when trying to quit smoking. For example, smokers who want to quit often try things like sucking on hard candy or chewing on a straw.

If you want to eliminate the bad habit of smoking, you have to make up your mind to quit and act on your decision. You have to be self-reliant, and believe in your ability to quit. You have to know that quitting is going to be hard, but worthwhile. By focusing on the reasons why quitting smoking can be beneficial to you, you may be able to find the willpower to beat the habit. You have to respect yourself enough to bring about positive changes in your life. No matter how difficult it may be to ignore your nicotine cravings, if you are self-reliant, you can beat them. Willpower is the key to quitting smoking, but to have willpower, you must first know and like yourself for who you are and be self-reliant enough to stick to behavior patterns that will let you make the positive changes that will lead to your ultimate happiness. Break your old habits.

Breaking Habits with to Self reliance and Constructive Changes

Breaking habits is hard to do for some of us. At what time you use your own guide to build self-reliance skills to make constructive changes it brings you good rewards. When we focus on breaking old habits that slow us down, it often rewards us with success.

Most people grow older and form some kind of habit that we just cannot seem to break. Many habits such as smoking and overeating are harmful to our health. When trying to break habits that we have it takes time, patience, and positive thinking. Using will help us to relieve the stress that causes up to overeat or smoke.

There are many guides to help lead us down the road for success in breaking bad habits.

As we begin to journey down the road use your self-talking skills to help relieve more stress that is about to hit us head on.

Everyone has daily stress. There is nothing we can do but learn to thrive on him or her. There is some stress that we can eliminate to help lessen the heavy load when breaking bad habits. Use your self-talk and ask yourself why you feel the need to smoke or binge eats. Think about the consequences of your actions. Where does a cigarette or more food get you when feeling the urge?

Let me pass on some guides that may help you to stop smoking or overeating.

Once you've done some self-talk with positive thinking to relieve them from your mind write how you can change them so they don't interfere in making constructive changes for breaking bad habits.

Writing goals for not smoking or overeating will help guide you through the rough times. Make your goals reasonable by not smoking for one day than lengthen the time out for 3 or 4 days. Set you goals to include your eating habits to get control so you do not gain weight that usually comes with quitting the habit of smoking. Set goals for an exercise plan to work off the weight gain you may have.

When you quit smoking, it is usually going to make you gain weight that can be very depressing. As you gain weight, you want to smoke. Including an exercise plan in you goals will help the weight gain and relieve stress that is bound to hit. Learn to thrive on stress so that you can reach your goals successfully.

As you reach each goal for not smoking and exercising, reward yourself with something special. It is a special time when you manage to stop smoking even for one day.

Learning meditation skills will help relieve stress from not smoking and overeating. When you meditate it will help you focus on you self-reliance to make constructive changes. You are bound to become stressed. The stress may encourage your need to smoke or eat heavily. Review your goals.

Reread your plans as a reminding for you to gain control of your life and put them bad habits behind you.

Think positive every time you get the urge to smoke or eat by using your guides for making constructive changes. Remind yourself using your self-reliance skills how much healthier you will be without all these bad habits.

Review your list often. When you see that you have achieved a goal, check it and reward you with something you enjoy. Be successful with guides and plans to relieve stressors that can be controlled as well the ones that come with breaking habits. Guides and plans will get you a long way to living a healthier life.

Conclusion:

Diet is the largest growing concern in the world today. Whether it's too much or too little, there is a massive problem when it comes to the food we eat. While it seems somewhat unimportant, it's one of the major players in providing us with happiness. You may think that it doesn't matter what you eat, as long as you're eating, but this is a very untrue statement. The better and more balanced your diet, the better you will feel, the clearer you will think and the more positive your outlook will become.

You can use this guide to start you on your way to eating better and eating smarter. Because you're new and healthy lifestyle choices, your mind will flow better, your ideas will become more focused and practical, your outlook on life will become more positive and your stress will decline. Not to mention that the state of your health will improve drastically,

The thing most neglected among teenagers and young adults in today's world is nutrition. People don't get the recommended nutrients they need to provide them with a clear head and a functioning body.

Take some initiative next time your in the grocery store. Instead of getting that greasy, fried chicken... pick up a package of boneless, skinless chicken breast that you can cook up. It's just as tasty and amazingly nutritious.

Instead of having four or five cups of coffee a day, substitute your caffeine addiction with herbal teas. They're invigorating and contain many natural ingredients to stimulate the mind without the harmful effects of caffeine.

Because you have started to replace the foods in your life that pose problems, such as greasy burgers and fries with lean beef and baked potatoes, you will see your body becoming healthier. With a healthy body comes a healthy mind. You will no longer find yourself stumbling over words, trying to remember what you were supposed to be doing, sitting at a desk for five minutes trying to think up a suitable synonym. These will all be outdated. Your intellect and potential will skyrocket with the implementation of a balanced, nutritional diet.

It seems too simple even be true; can I really bring about positive and constructive changes in my life simply by changing what I eat? It may sound silly, but it's true! The hundreds of preservatives and additives in today's food clog our systems. The prevent proper blood flow, clog arteries, increase the risk of heart attacks, build up fat and just make us feel overall bad about ourselves.

This is what prevents our success, a bad self-image. You will not be able to rely on and trust yourself if you perceive yourself in a negative light. Eating healthier will help you fix that. You will begin to feel better about the choices you make. The nutrients you take in will help you feel energized and motivated; you will be ready to face those problems and that stress instead of trying to forget about it until it piles up on you. Your lethargy will be gone and will be replaced with a new sense of pride about yourself and the initiative to bring change.

Now you must realize this can't be done overnight. Changing your lifestyle requires dedication. You will have to change not just your eating habits but your exercise habits as well. Combine that salad with a jog, you'll feel twice as good; Have those carrots as a snack in-between tennis matches. It doesn't take much, just a little initiative and positive thought.

Once you achieve these, you can begin your goal to a healthier lifestyle, which will ultimately propel you forward into making constructive changes in your life. When you feel good about yourself, you can then start to rely on yourself.

CPSIA information can be obtained
at www.ICGtesting.com
Printed in the USA
BVHW070954200421
605389BV00005B/1544

9 781801 549936